# VOICES OF PAIN AND VOICES OF HOPE

## *Students Speak about Racism*

### SECOND EDITION

**Jerome Rabow**
University of California, Los Angeles

*With the Assistance of*
**Michelle Charness**

*Forewords by*
**Mark Chesler**
*and*
**James Fenelon**

**KENDALL/HUNT PUBLISHING COMPANY**
4050 Westmark Drive    Dubuque, Iowa 52002

*This book is dedicated to my grandchildren:*
*Matthew Samuel Rabow, Zacahary Tyler Rabow,*
*Lucie Carolina Berman and Liliana Jeanette Berman.*

*In memoriam to :*
*Ruth J. Alatorre and Yvette Villalobos, who died before they*
*could finish the wonderful things they started, and*
*Paul Page who fulfilled his promise to Oskar Schindler.*

*And*

*To the thousands of students who have trusted me*
*with their fears and the hope that comes from healing.*
*All of you have shown me that America can*
*come closer to its ideals of freedom and equality.*
*May all the children on campuses throughout the country*
*come to understand that racism*
*need not be part and parcel of American life.*

A portion of all royalties shall be given
towards a scholarship fund for deserving students at UCLA,
and California State University, Northridge

# CONTENTS

# FOREWORD

*by Mark Chesler, Ph. D*
*Professor of Sociology, University of Michigan*
*Executive Director of Community Resources Ltd.*

Is race salient for university students? Rabow and the students in this book say absolutely "yes." But how is it salient: for whom, under what conditions, and in what ways? This work indicates that it is salient for everyone, all the time, and in both overt and covert ways. By using the ideas of "painting" and the "paintbrush" Jerome Rabow provides us with an intriguing metaphor for the process of social construction that reifies race while it mystifies it, that tries to cover the realities of real racial interaction with pretty words and images.

Here, in the midst of one of the nation's most cosmopolitan communities and universities, in a very racially mixed environment, we see laid bare the myriad issues young people (especially, but certainly not exclusively young people) of different racial backgrounds and memberships face on a daily basis. More importantly, and in the words presented in this brief volume, we see and hear what we often do not acknowledge.

We hear White students expressing their ignorance, their confusion, and their guilt or concern as they confront their own prejudicial views of others and as they hear how their speech and behavior cause pain to others.

We hear White students struggling to understand their symbolic and material privilege, with the knowledge that they help to paint the world and others in ways that mask reality.

We hear students of color reporting their own confusion and pain at the words and deeds expressed by White students and institutions, and at the ways they are painted into corners by assumptions others make about them.

We also hear students of color discussing the ways they, too, paint themselves and others.

We hear biracial and multiracial students struggle to find paints that truly represent them as they look for their unique place in a Black and White world.

We hear how all these students try to talk with and hear one another and come to new ways of thinking and relating to themselves and others.

And we hear, perhaps with amazement, what one daring faculty member can accomplish in a classroom . . . and what students of varied backgrounds will let him accomplish with them.

The messages that these students and this scholar share are applicable to students and teachers and adults in schools and colleges and communities and corporations throughout our nation.

As Rabow says, the gift of this class is that "It allowed students to analyze their own identities, with an emphasis on the internalized racial and ethnic stereotypes of themselves and others." The examination of "your racism and mine" makes it clear that "We have been taught to paint and we all have painted." As they understand and apply the painting metaphor these students, and all of us, know we must move beyond simplistic notions of a colorblind world.

This work shows us what a committed and courageous person—a teacher—can do. As much as Rabow showcases the students with whom he worked, he manifests his own innovative and antiracist abilities in several important ways. For one, he shows us that one can teach in a daring and innovative way; that instructors can enter the contentious and often frightening world of race relations by inviting students to engage in deep and intimate explorations of their experiences and views. In the midst of many campus programs that are developing small-group interracial dialogues, Rabow shows us that one can also do this in a large class. For another, Rabow shows us that as a "justice worker," as an older, straight, White man who is a scholar and teacher committed to antiracism and social justice, he can test the boundaries of these group distinctions. He explores, engages, and sometimes crosses these boundaries with his students, successfully inviting them to share with one another and with him their deeply held secrets, fears and hopes about their racial worlds. And finally, Rabow shows us how doing research is part of the doing of everyday life; without substantial federal or foundation grants and resources, he gathers and analyzes data in ways that illuminate these students (and our) racial experiences. This rich descriptive research, with its extensive quote material, allows us to see into young people's minds and hearts. It is a welcome addition to the mounds of academic work on race that so often fail to reflect people's everyday realities and thus fails to touch or educate us deeply.

In this book Jerome Rabow and these students show us how to see the way we all paint the world and thus contribute to the maintenance of racism and social injustice. It is at once a descriptive ethnography, an analytic window into the lives of people struggling to find their place within a racialized society, a ray of hope that dialogic encounters with others may generate new insights and behaviors, and a marvelous story of a daring and successful teaching enterprise. As this gifted teacher teaches he learns, as he and these students uncover their worlds they provide insight into our own. This book is a primer for students and teachers everywhere, for people of all racial groups who wish to understand their own and others' worlds, and for all of us who wish to see beneath the layers of paint.

This brief volume should be very useful in social science classes, and in the applied disciplines of education, social work, business, and public health. Moreover, it should be especially useful in those collegiate and community efforts to create intergroup dialogues and to teach about pathways to social justice. It is a good read and a model of good work.

*—Mark Chesler*
*Professor of Sociology at the University of Michigan*
*and Executive Director of Community Resources Ltd.*

Poem

Shh
Listen to the voices
Journey through the guts and souls of the other
Discover the other is no other than yourself sketched upside down
By you
With my brush
On her canvas
With his paint
And let's turn this world around
Recover childhood innocence
Find old crayons
Color this world new
You!

*—Derrick I. M. Gilbert (a.k.a. D-Knowledge)*, Assistant Professor of Afroamerican and African Studies, Residential College; Adjunct, Department of Sociology, University of Michigan, Ann Arbor

# FOREWORD TO SECOND EDITION

*Voices of Pain and Voices of Hope* has proven to be an excellent choice for my large-section class called "Race and Racism". It not only gives "voice" to students that our class can relate to, but seems to stimulate "voice" from the class participants. Students need to internalize some of the discussion, especially as the course develops, and this book does that wonderfully by allowing them to read about and respond to comments by those in roughly the same situation.

The book is perfect for my course, because first we deal with the historical origins of race and racism, moving into understanding the institutionalization and reproduction of race and racism in the second third of the course.

One of the many unexpected benefits of this book is that it provides a stimulus for students to reflect on their own experiences. In the third part of the class, students begin to voice their reactions to the "other" in terms of subordinates and dominants. This conceptualization allows for safer discussions even as it gets to the heart of the matter. In our diverse classrooms, especially when dealing with topics like this, hearing and responding to those too often marginalized and quieted can assist antiracism struggles on many fronts. Perhaps the greatest benefit, in times when many claim they are "colorblind" or that "racism is dead and gone," this book firmly establishes that for many students of racial minority background, the issues are real and ongoing. That forces all of us to deal with, at the very least, our experiences and feelings.

*James V. Fenelon*
*Associate Professor, Sociology*
*California State University San Bernardino*

# PRAISE

### for *Voices of Pain and Voices of Hope*

"Professor Jerome Rabow has put together an extremely valuable book which demonstrates that, despite much progress since the civil rights movement of the 1960s, racism in its many guises is still alive. In addition to the convincing evidence for the persistence of this long-standing American dilemma, *Voices of Pain and Voices of Hope* provides a method for dealing with the problem. College courses in which students express their individual experiences with racism—both orally and in writing—become the place for meaningful dialogue in which real attitude change takes place. The many quotations from students, give a convincing firsthand feel for the problem as well as demonstrating the process of confrontation with prejudicial attitudes in their living form. An impressive and psychologically insightful work."

> **—Louis Breger, Ph.D.** Professor of Psychoanalytic Studies, Emeritus at California Institute of Technology, founding president of the Institute of Contemporary Psychoanalysis, author of *Freud: Darkness in the Midst of Vision* (Wiley & Sons, 2000)

"Rabow and his students have tackled the topic of racial relations in a way that finally makes the disparities between Whites and other ethnicities in American society self-evident. This is the raw, emotional, human experience of racism, from the perspective of both the oppressors and the oppressed (who, we learn, can sometimes be one and the same). Through the experiences of his students, Rabow elucidates the dominance of White culture in example after example, until it becomes impossible to deny. Though scholarly and academic, this work has the heart and soul that are missing from many theoretically or empirically focused discussions of race. The end result is a dispiriting, but ultimately hopeful perspective that calls each of us to consider what being an American really means."

> **—Terri D. Conley, Ph.D.** Social Science Research Council Fellow and Adjunct Assistant Professor of Psychology, California State University, Northridge

"*Voices of Pain and Voices of Hope* is required reading for anyone wanting to learn about contemporary racism and how this form of domination is learned, practiced, and comes to have widespread and deep impacts in our society. Rabow communicates and illustrates through the writings of college students the multiple dimensions and dynamics of racism in the lives of young people and in their relationships with each other and with their elders. The book creatively and effectively describes the experiences and feelings of college students about the meaning of race and racism in their every-day-lives. Using a powerful metaphor of a paintbrush and bucket of white paint that is wielded for the most part by White Americans, readers are skillfully and engagingly taught about a topic that is all too often ignored or dealt with in vague and otherwise confusing ways. Based on how it has impacted me, I strongly recommend that you read *Voices of Pain and Voices of Hope*."

> —**James Crowfoot, Ph.D.** Professor Emeritus of Natural Resources and Urban and Regional Planning, Dean Emeritus of the School of Natural Resources and Environment, University of Michigan at Ann Arbor, former President of Antioch College, Yellow Springs, Ohio, and author of *Challenging Racism and Promoting Multiculturalism in Higher Education* (forthcoming)

"This extremely perceptive book succinctly illustrates how today's new racism undermines our talk about tolerance, understanding, and social justice. Students and the parents of students who wish to understand what growing up in America is about should read this book. It is especially important for teachers at all levels of our educational system."

> —**Carole Donahue,** Los Angeles Unified School District Academic Mentor Coordinator

"The list of social critics and pundits who claim to speak for students confronting racial and ethnic tensions on college campuses grows longer each year, but there is nothing quite so convincing as the voices of students themselves. Rabow's book provides these students with a megaphone, and they use it to address the complexity of issues that engage them—thereby avoiding the cliches that have so often rendered 'the debate about race on campus' stale and sterile. This is, in contrast, a breath of fresh air."

> —**Troy Duster,** Professor, New York University

"*Voices* is both street smart and theoretically sophisticated. It allows the students to speak in their own voices and their stories are often moving even to veterans like myself. What they have to say resonates beyond the campus and demands to be heard everywhere."

—**Howard J. Ehrlich,** Director of the Prejudice Institute and editor of *Perspectives,* the newsletter of prejudice, ethnoviolence, and social policy

"This book conclusively refutes the notion that racism is dead. Brilliantly probing racial matters, Jerome Rabow examines accounts from college student journals. White, Black, Asian, Latino, Indian, and multiracial students grapple with the realities of racial oppression that many White Americans deny. Ever painful, often profound, the accounts offer major insights about the persisting tragedy of White racism. One senses here great pessimism, as students of color document much painful discrimination by teachers, clerks, and the police. But there is hope too, for in their journals many students of all backgrounds show they have learned to respect others and to work assertively for the elimination of racism."

—**Joe Feagin,** Graduate Research Professor, University of Florida, and author of *Racist America* (Routledge, 2000)

"*Voices of Pain* belongs in the public discourse on where this nation is on issues affecting race and ethnicity. I am excited to see this publication and would urge all Americans to read this work and ponder its contents."

—California State Assemblymember, **Jackie Goldberg**

"Is the American 'melting pot' working? Is racism and prejudice on the wane? Not according to Professor Rabow's students, who reveal in this provocative new book how old ideas and attitudes about race and difference persist in our new multicultural, multiethnic world."

—**Neal Goldberg, L. C. S. W.** and author

"*Voices* offers compelling evidence that should challenge those who believe that racist actions are infrequent and only an annoyance. Professor Rabow, through the voices of his students, demonstrates the high degree of regularity, the prevalence and the pain of racism for children of color, as well as the sense of privilege that develops among whites. This book also shows that when the pain is brought into the open and conflicts unfold, it then becomes possible for resolutions to occur. This book should be read by all of us who teach and care about the future of American race relations."

—**Morgan Hatch,** Teacher, Los Angeles Unified School District

*"Voices of Pain and Voices of Hope* chronicles the experiences that University of California Los Angeles students have with racism and prejudice and the pain it invokes. Racism is alive and well in U.S. society. Professor Rabow documents the process in which students recognize that they are racist. All too often individuals perceive the "other" as racist and do not consider the "self" as racist. It is vital that this self-realization occurs so that racial ethnic differences can be embraced rather than shunned. The transformation that students experienced in this course is a nascent beginning. The challenge they confront is to go beyond the classroom and affect change in the broader society. This book encapsulates the hope that someday racial ethnic differences will be embraced and appreciated, that racism will be dead and that America will fulfill its promise of participation and hope for all."

> **—Anthony Hernandez, Ph.D.** Associate Professor, Charter College of Education, California State University Los Angeles

*"Voices of Pain and Voices of Hope* is a must-read text for students of race relations. A racial mosaic of privilege and disadvantage, Rabow's students come alive before our very eyes in this timely work. We hear their voices loud and clear. They chronicle the pain engendered by continuing racial oppression in America, but still manage to provide us with reasons to hope for a better future."

> **—Darnell M. Hunt, Ph.D.** Director of the Center for African American Studies, Professor of Sociology, University of California, Los Angeles. Author of *O. J. Simpson Fact and Fictions* (Cambridge Press, 1999)

*"Voices of Pain and Voices of Hope* demonstrates our burden of bigotry and how it pervades American life. This book can help us become conscious of our own racism and privilege. With increased awareness Americans may be more willing to take responsibility for the tragic state of race relations in our society."

> **—Melinda Hurst,** Los Angels Unified School District Teacher, Retired; Institutional Review Board, University of Southern California, Los Angeles, California

"When articulate college students dig deeply into their experience of race and speak honestly about it, the result is a revealing picture of the challenge of diversity in America."

> **—Rosabeth Moss Kanter,** Harvard Business School, best-selling author of *Evolve!* and *World Class*

"A literary documentary, *Voices* walks the reader through the real-life experiences of individuals who have personally been affected by the racism that covertly exists in America today. Prof. Rabow challenges the old boy's club, thereby breaking free from his silent privilege and adding to the canon on diversity. Having participated in the class as an undergraduate student at UCLA, I was reminded of the voices of my own journey and understanding of privilege and oppression. Currently, I teach and work in the area of diversity and I recognize the necessity of this book. It is a must read for all who teach race and who wish to have an impact on their students' understanding of the chasms that exist between races and ethnic groups. Honest, candid, and real, the reader is exposed to the truths of the voices of oppressed and privileged individuals."

——**Ani Karayan, Ph.D.** Adjunct Professor, Department of Psychology, Antioch University, Los Angeles

"Jerome Rabow's *Voices of Pain and Voices of Hope: Students Speak About Racism* is an enormously impressive work. It is an original and daring approach to understanding the meaning of race among today's college students. At large universities like UCLA and Berkeley the faculty for the most part "deal" with simmering racial tensions and pain by ignoring them, hoping that it will all just go away. Rabow in contrast puts the confrontation of our feelings about race and racism at the core of his teaching, confronting rather than avoiding resentments and insensitivity that students bring with them to the Big U, which, I fear, we as professors only exacerbate. "Voices" is based on a series of quite special courses Rabow taught in the past few years in which, in addition to the usual readings and assignments, students kept journals of their reactions to and reflections on the often very emotional in-class goings on. Race, gender and sexual preference become intertwined in ways that many older academics will find discomforting, reminding us that, above all, these are the thoughts and feelings of individuals caught up in many dimensions of trauma and conflict, but in America the racial dimension is always paramount. I recommend this book to anyone concerned with the growing racial divide in the United States; I especially recommend it to those who do not see this growing divide."

——**David Lopez,** Professor of Sociology at UCLA

"This book can be appreciated on two levels. At one level, it is a record of a White, male professor's discovery of the pervasiveness of racism even decades after the civil rights movement. At a second level, it is a collection of college students' accounts of either surviving the pain of racism or coming to realize the privileges they had never noticed. Many professors fear direct and concrete debates on race in their classroom, but

Professor Rabow voluntarily chose a method of instruction that would expose and interrogate the biases of himself and his students. *Voices of Pain* emerged from this experience, and documents how prejudice continues to operate in everyday life. It's a book you won't soon forget."

—**Laura L. Miller,** Social Scientist, RAND

"My recent work with outreach to middle and high school students from educationally disadvantaged schools and communities suggests that the school environment directly impacts how we learn and succeed in life. A simple "commitment to diversity" is insufficient for involving all students in their education. This book points to the urgent need to create an environment on our campuses that embraces differences rather than tolerating them, an essential ingredient to teaching and learning."

—**Jane S. Permaul,** Chief Operating Officer, UCLA, Outreach, Assistant Vice Chancellor Emeritus

"*Voices of Pain and Voices of Hope* is an insightful book about how college students learn about, experience, and struggle with racial prejudice. Based on the personal journals that students kept as they took Rabow's course, the book is an excellent answer to those who mistakenly argue that we are in a postracist society. Students in courses dealing with race and ethnic diversity will easily identify with the material since it is based on the experiences of their peers."

—**Fred L. Pincus,** Co-Editor of *Race and Ethnic Conflict,* 2nd edition (Westview, 1999) and affiliated with the University of Maryland Baltimore County

"This work represents an important contribution to all of the voices that must be heard as we struggle with issues of difference, conflict, and change. This book is part text, part classroom exercise, and part life lesson. It is a necessary addition to any personal reading list and any professional library."

—**Jorja Prover,** Adjunct Professor, UCLA Department of Social Welfare

"Dr. Rabow casts a light on the dark side of cultural issues impacting therapy. The wounds of racism not only help shape the individual's identity, these wounds also give rise to deep emotions. Dr. Rabow demonstrates that it is not only important to know the client's experiences of racism; it is imperative the clinician be aware of his or her own prejudices which may affect the therapist's perception of the client . . . and the client's perception of the therapist."

—**Carolyn J. Roberts, Ph.D.** MFT

"Therapists, parents, and students should read this work. As a therapist, I found Dr. Rabow's research valuable in reminding us that the road to self-acceptance is still littered with the obstacles of racism. He brilliantly illustrates the connection between self-acceptance and acceptance of others, and paints the destructive picture of both the false sense of superiority and inferiority that racism imposes. The book illustrates how healing can occur when diversity is not just tolerated but embraced."

　—**Toby Salter,** MA, MFT

"*Voices of Pain and Voices of Hope* is a highly readable and wonderful contribution to the large and growing literature on race and racism in America. By exploring the journals of college students from one of America's most multiethnic campuses, it allows the reader to get an inside-out grasp of the depth, breadth, and power of racism as it is experienced in everyday life. While America has certainly made great progress in confronting the dreadful scourge of racial oppression, this book makes it painfully clear just how much serious work still needs to be done. This is a very valuable book for anyone interested in gaining insight into the complex, multifaceted, and subtle dynamics of race in American society."

　—**Professor James Sidanius,** Professor of Psychology and Political Science, The University of California, Los Angeles, author of *Social Dominance: An Intergroup Theory of Social Hierarchy and Oppression* (Cambridge University Press, 2001)

"Professor Jerome Rabow takes on the tough issues of racism in the university, exposing its many dimensions in the lives of young people today. His approach to teaching is brave, sensitive, and audacious. This book lets students speak of their own experience, revealing to us as readers both their pain and their hope. It is an inspiring work of pedagogy that further advances the dialogue on race and racism in America. We all have a great deal to learn from these voices."

　—**Jill Stein,** Director of Sociology, Dept. of Sociology and Anthropology, Santa Barbara City College

"From the manuscript we find out that all is not well in one of the nation's most ethnically diverse campuses. Through these voices on the ground, we see that racism for this new college generation is not so subtle and race is not so unimportant as many would claim, even among UCLA students, who are selected for their desire to attend a diverse campus and their purported greater intellect. We learn that the incidents of intolerance that these students endured can be deeply scarring and enduring. These issues, although central in the life of many of our students, are probably unbeknownst to most professors. If we had a way to formally train college professors as educators, then I think this should become a required book. The book is short and its presentational style makes it an easy read but the central message is well driven and supported with engaging passages from the students."

  —**Eddie Telles,** Professor of Sociology, University of California Los Angeles

*"Voices of Pain and Voices of Hope* explores our struggles with racism in a vital way: from the inside out. This book teaches that the social psychology of racism is based, above all, on fear and vulnerability. Racism can be challenged in important ways by facing up to the shameful privilege it defends and the inner pain it masks. Rabow's students can be our teachers. This book will make a valuable contribution to courses in sociology, psychology, education, and ethnic studies."

  —**Howard Winant,** University of California, Santa Barbara, author of *The World Is a Ghetto*

# PREFACE

This book is the outcome of a class I taught at UCLA which I subtitled "Your Racism and Mine." Its vision and words are taken from the journals of my students. Their voices poignantly exemplify experiences with current-day prejudice and racism and the pain that these injustices invoke. The idea for the class grew out of my response to Troy Duster's work regarding University of California, Berkeley undergraduate students (Duster, 1992, 1993). Specifically, Duster had been invited by the Berkeley administration to understand the racial and ethnic experience of undergraduates during their 4 years of education at this elite, public university. His conclusion was that, after 4 years, students felt increased levels of bitterness, hostility, and suspicion towards members of other racial ethnic groups. In other words, the Berkeley students felt more racially divided and antagonistic and more deeply committed to their stereotypes upon leaving college than when they had first arrived. This finding was astounding considering that many of these same students had come to Berkeley with the desire of being in a multicultural and multiracial environment. They were actually looking forward to living with and experiencing diversity. I was very upset upon reading what happened to students at Berkeley, but also knew that many of my own students at UCLA were feeling the same way. I had heard stories and anecdotes about cruel racial slurs, homophobic responses, and sexist philosophy experienced by my students in their collegiate surroundings. After recognizing that little was being done on my campus to help "bring students together," I decided to teach a class focusing on racism which would also include discussions on the topics of sexism, elitism, and homophobia. I was particularly interested in demonstrating to students how they themselves, as I, were "racist." With this goal in mind came the vision, birth, and development of the class, "Your Racism and Mine."

While I taught this first class by myself, two colleagues in particular were instrumental in providing me with useful insight in charting unfamiliar territory. Specifically, Professor Mark Chesler at the University of Ann Arbor Michigan, and Professor Beverly Tatum who was then a Professor at Mount Holyoke College in Massachusetts and who is now President of Spelman College, Georgia, collaborated with me in creating a reading list. This list was excellent and was appreciated by the students.

During the course of teaching the class for the first time, I discovered through my interactions with the students that my ignorance was profound. My mistakes were countless, but fortunately my students tolerated my blunders, insensitivity, and naiveté. To begin with, I was ignorant of the significant needs and experiences of biracial students and their individual issues. The uniqueness of being multiracial and the particular ramifications that accompany it had never occurred to me.

I had expected that Blacks, Latinos, and Asians would feel some bond towards each other as a result of their common experiences with racism— that they would feel similarly in their deep suspicions and anger towards Caucasians. Indeed, though these diverse groups of students shared feelings of mistrust and anger towards Whites, I was completely unprepared for the animosity that these groups felt towards each other.

Furthermore, I was naive and insensitive toward my own issues with sexism; female undergraduate students in the class could not sense my commitment to being supportive of their struggles. Indeed, my ignorance prevented me from seeing the subtle and not so subtle ways in which I benefited from being a White, heterosexual male and how the privileges that accrued to me from those characteristics influenced my teaching.

Moreover, I had no knowledge of the biases and prejudice towards Arabic, Middle Eastern, and immigrant students. These expressions of racism turned virulent after 9/11 and inspired a new chapter, Chapter 7 for this second edition. Additionally, I was unaware of the prejudice and racism that students of color experience on a daily basis as well as the pain they inflict upon themselves. When I say unaware, I mean that I was shocked to discover and hear about the prior, systematic, constant, everyday, in-your-face discrimination, as well as the subtle, unconscious racism that had affected students. They exposed me to the prejudice and racism they experienced before college and the prejudice and racism that was part of their university experience. The prejudice and racism was in their classrooms, professors' offices, dorms, walkways, campus eating areas, barbershops, and the nearby department stores that make a good living from student purchases.

Muddying the waters even further was the fact that I was unclear as to how I could work with White students who could potentially feel frightened, guilty, and shut out by the focus of the class. I was also concerned that they might not be able to acknowledge that they supported racism either implicitly or explicitly.

Apparently, my own naiveté had led me to believe that racism was lessening in this country. I see now that this erroneous belief was based on my privilege and my own experiences with witnessing the great events of the 1960s: the desegregation of major facilities and institutions in America; the passing of the Civil Rights Bill, and the start of 30 years of affirmative action.

All of my inexperience was superceded by my conviction that open discussion and dialogue would help eliminate stereotypes and prejudice. I envisioned singing "We Shall Overcome" at the end of class while we held hands, as if this would somehow symbolize a healing of wounds, past and present.

Despite my deficits, during the birth and development of this first class, students ultimately were able to create open dialogue. Though many of the students said they believed that race was the most important issue in their lives, no one had ever encouraged them to talk seriously about it with others. In this first class, students actually had the chance to talk about privileges, biases, and prejudices, and their own participation in those practices. They talked about the jokes they had repeated or let slide and about parental teachings, hatreds, angers, and fears. They talked about their life in the dorms, their experiences in searching for apartments, shopping, and the daily energies that went into thinking about race. Not withstanding all the errors I made in this 6-week long summer school class, on the last day, two students who had spent 5 weeks first ignoring, then glaring, and finally screaming at one another, walked out talking to each other. One was a Korean student who had stood on a rooftop with an AK47 during the Los Angeles rebellion of 1992, prepared to kill anyone who threatened to damage his father's store. The other student was an African American male who had forcefully and brilliantly debated that the L.A. revolt was due to frustration, broken promises, and racism.

Students asserted in their evaluations that they had learned a lot from my course. This encouraged me to do it again. I knew that I had to learn much more about racism, diversity, multiculturalism, and working with both individuals who were motivated to change their attitudes and behavior and also with those who saw nothing wrong with the current state of race relations in the United States. Fortunately, my interest in learning was supported by Professor Claudia Mitchell-Kernan, Vice Chancellor of Academic Affairs, and Dean of the Graduate Division, who gave me a grant to travel and spend 4 days at a multicultural training program in Washington, D.C.

As a result of this first class, I also realized that I, as a White male, could not do it alone. A class is not just a class when we teach race in the United States. Knowing one's subject matter is critical, of course, but what also matters is a teaching arrangement that exemplifies and embodies the very essence of what you are trying to achieve.[1] I wanted to demonstrate a

---

[1] There is some solid evidence that some characteristics of professors make it impossible for some students to identify with their instructors (Gerschick, 1995): Race is obviously one which would matter more in some classes than others. For readers interested in what "White teachers" need to learn about racism before they teach, see "We Can't Teach What We Don't Know" by Gary R. Howard, 1999.

model of deep collaboration and trust by racially different people. Additionally, I wanted to show that Whites and non-Whites, men and women, could share a common and compelling interest—the understanding and reduction of prejudice and racism.

For my second attempt at reducing and confronting prejudice and racism in the course, I co-instructed with Derrick Gilbert, an African American male graduate student who has since earned his Ph.D., and Ruth Alatorre, a Latina and former student in the Sociology Graduate Program. My departmental chair, Robert Emerson, was able to give Derrick and Ruth a modest stipend, and together we were able to initiate dialogues and create an atmosphere in which issues could be explored more deeply. Our three different backgrounds and personalities gave us the ability to reach and touch a wide range of students. And all the while I kept learning. Later, a new Chair, Ivan Zeleyni, also found funds to support my collective teaching effort.

After a time, I began to get a sense of the paths students would take with themselves and with other groups. I began to understand the major issues and concerns that needed to be addressed. Further, I introduced readings by Tatum (1997), McIntosh (1998), Miller (1998), and discovered an excellent book of readings by Paula Rothenberg (1998b). I utilized DuBois (1903, 1995) to establish how privilege is a critical concept and how internalized oppression, originally called "double consciousness," played out in the lives of students of color. I came to understand how the multiracial students posed a challenge to our fundamental thoughts about racial groupings and "race" as a construct, and how sexual identity remained the deepest barrier to understanding, trust, and alliance. All the while, I never stopped learning from my students. These were individuals who would share their deepest pains around racism and sexism, students who told us how they were stuck in hatred and in anger, and who despite periods of rage and bitterness, hoped for something different and decent.

As is the case with charting new territory, there were often trouble spots, failures, and feelings of confusion and impotence. Derrick, Ruth, and I had ongoing discussions about these problems. When particular groups of students got upset or frustrated, my colleagues could work with their identity groups as I worked with mine. Always there was Mark Chelser, who never failed to provide guidance and support. Later, Jill Stein, a lecturer in the Sociology Department at UCLA, recipient of the university's Distinguished Teaching Award, Executive Director of the Leroy Neiman Center for the Study of American Society and Culture, and currently the Director of Sociology, Department of Sociology and Anthropology, Santa Barbara City College became a valuable partner. When she joined our teaching team, she strongly challenged the place of sexism in the class. She forced Derrick and me to think through this issue and to understand the place of sexism in a class on racism. When Trang Minh Le joined Professor Gilbert and me in our teaching efforts, she made an invaluable contribution to students' development and understanding. Trang also became a vital part of facilitator training. Ani Karayan also joined the class and was an excellent sounding board as well as a trainer of the facilitators.

In the end, mostly, I learned from students and their voices—voices in lectures, in small groups, and in their journals—voices that responded to films, books, and the personal experiences of other students. The closest I can bring you to these wonderful people and their experiences is through the writing in their journals. It is these journals which inspired this book. We want you, the reader, to know about the deep, ongoing, and everyday racism that is so prevalent in our country. For those readers who know firsthand that racism exists and is extensive, we hope that you will still find something in these pages that takes you to a deeper level of understanding and appreciation of the complicated dynamics of racism. For others who may be less aware, we hope that you will be able to open your minds and hearts to the voices you hear in this book. Perhaps most importantly, we hope that schools and universities begin to tackle the issue of racism in the United States in a way that is more realistic. Celebrating Martin Luther King's birthday, Cinco de Mayo, awarding reparations to Japanese Americans, and building Holocaust memorials is not sufficient for uncovering the chasms that exist between groups. Nor will a single day of dialogue address the anger, frustration, confusion, and denial that exists within individuals and between groups. Although this 10-week class somewhat closed the divide amongst diverse groups, it was not a guarantee that the changes that occurred would be able to endure in the "fresh air of racism." If anything, we hope this book makes clear the depth and scope of a problem that is not going to just go away.

The excerpts in this book are taken from the journals that students wrote as part of my UCLA Sociology course called "Inter-Group Conflict and Prejudice" (Sociology 160). These journals are remarkable for their depth and clarity, pain and hope. The journals would not have been so personal if the class had not been so personal; thus, a few words need to be said about the class. The purposes of the class became clearer and clearer to me each time I taught it. Now I announce it as a class designed to explore racism, classism, sexism, and homophobia and to focus on how prejudice, stereotypes, guilt, and fear play out in students' daily lives and in the classroom. I always start my class by stating that everyone in the class is racist, sexist, and homophobic, including myself. I tell my students that simply reading about and analyzing racism, sexism, or classism is "safe" because most classes on racism in the academy treat these structures as if they are only "out there" in the world and are not operative in our classrooms. I now take the more demanding position and let students understand why it is more productive to see, hear, and feel how racism, sexism, elitism, and homophobia are "right here" on our campus, in our classrooms, and in our heads, attitudes, feelings, and behavior. There are many ways to illustrate this for students. I may ask for recent examples of racism or sexism to illustrate this point. I may also suggest that the students might believe that they are better than others because of a college degree (elitism), or that they are better because they are heterosexual, or "prettier" because they have lighter skin. It is easy for students to confirm this with personal examples. I try to make it explicit and clear that although racism and sexism operate within social structures, it is also the students who implement those structures in their classrooms, dormitories, and social lives. They feel prejudice, often believing it and sometimes acting on it.

To engender this understanding and to encourage dialogue, I approached these issues from a social, psychological, and interpersonal perspective, and I taught them in the most direct, interactive, and personal way possible. My pedagogical style demanded that the classroom be a safe environment in which the students were respected by all. Students were encouraged to use "I" statements whenever possible and interruptions were discouraged. In this format, I encouraged students to challenge comments made by their classmates. Specifically, I wanted students to engage each other, and more often than not, they did. I attributed student transformations to this open and safe environment in which they were able to examine their deeper feelings, fears, and confusions. They were prompted to explore their own behavior and to establish a dialogue and discussion, and thus a sense of identification with each other. I know with some surety that not all students felt safe all of the time. For example, students "turned off" when they felt that a speaker was being strategic or self-pitying. Moreover, I could not always facilitate the discussion to move beyond the pain. People sometimes laughed at others; sometimes they yelled and scared others. In these instances, we needed to address the pain caused by laughter and the fear and shame caused by ridicule. The goal was always to accept and understand the "others'" subjectivity.

In addition to the active class participation, students were required to keep weekly journals in which they explored their feelings and reactions to the reading material, class lectures, films, guest speakers, and discussions. These journals, which are the data for this book, were designed to ensure students' anonymity and were accordingly read and analyzed by two graduate students who did not attend lectures. Journals were labeled only with student identification numbers and we believe that this double-blind reading also served as a safeguard to avoid any potential inclination to please the professor. A set of guidelines was presented to students so that they could understand that their grades did not depend upon adhering to a particular party line.

The data from this book comes from four sources. One source was the journals collected from Sociology 160, winter term, 1997. At the end of the class, students were asked on a separate sheet of paper whether they would permit use of journals in a book. Of the 127 who kept journals, 88 students gave written consent for the use of their material. The 39 journals that we were not allowed to cite[2] or quote, were also reviewed for any significant differences and deviations from the students who granted permission. Searching for differences was completed for another paper (Richardson, Reyes, & Rabow, 1998) and because none were found, we felt that we could also utilize the journals for this book without presenting a biased reporting of student voices.

Four student coders and the professor subsequently reviewed the 88 journals. All relevant recorded material was coded according to preestablished categories. Any material that could not be coded was brought to the group, which developed new categories so that all information could be utilized. The final coding system consisted of seven general categories: transformations, voices of pain, awareness of White privilege, internalized oppression, biracial students, consequences of pain, and awareness. Though the categories were exhaustive, they were not mutually exclusive. As I continued to teach the "race" class, I was stimulated to think about the issues of racial, gender, and sexual orientation, all identity issues, and how these needed to be included in the other classes I taught. I began adding readings on identity to my other classes.

A second source for this book was a class I taught in the spring of 1999, Education and Race. In this small seminar, students were given an optional assignment in which six questions regarding prejudice and stereotypes were posed. Again permission was asked, and of the 15 students who turned in papers only 2 students refused to provide us with permission.

The third and fourth sources of student quotes was obtained from the social psychology class that I taught in the summer of 2001 and the Honors Collegium, a class I taught in the spring of 2002. Students were asked specific questions about racial and gender identity and they also had a Web site where they participated in discussing the issues raised by the readings. Four questions were given to the students for each of the 5 weeks and these five assignments asked the students to relate their own personal experiences with respect to racism, sexism, domination, subordination, prejudice, and stereotyping. After the grades were posted, I went on the message board and requested permission to quote from their journals and Web-site posts. Thirty-two out of 34 students allowed me to quote their work.

One conceivable problem regarding these journals is the possibility that the comments reported by students are artifacts. The journals were not only self-reports but also self-reports that were to be graded. This could easily produce exaggeration of pain or positive changes. Because change was implied by the nature of the class, there may well have been exaggeration. Another factor that may have influenced comments in the journals was the professor. It would be naive to believe that students could not see the professor's biases reflected in lectures and films that were selected for viewing and the readings.

Nonetheless, there are six facts that should give the reader confidence that the journals were not exaggerations or adaptations to the classroom or the professor. First, many students verbally expressed negativity about the class. Some were unhappy about the racist practices in which their fellow students had engaged. For others, the class was described as a waste of time since "I already know about prejudice." There were students who did not believe others' experiences with racism and felt that their peers were exaggerating. These comments were expressed in lectures and in small groups apart from the professor. It is clear, then, that students felt free to challenge other students as well as the biases of the class. Second, students described not simply attitudes but actual behavior. Behavior is much less reactive than expressed attitudes. Third, having small-group discussions meant that students would be more likely to be consistent with what they wrote in their journals and what they said in their small, face-to-face groups. It would be more difficult to pontificate and lecture in these small groups, which were set up to avoid posturing and required intellectual and personal explorations of the readings (Rabow, Radcliffe-Vasile, Charness, & Kipperman, 1999). Fourth, since the professor neither graded papers nor participated in small-group discussions, students were aware that they could not please the professor in their journals. Negative sentiments were expressed not only in the journals and lectures, but also during the small-group discussions organized for the explicit purposes of encouraging co-operation and face-to-face encounters with peers involved in the class. Also, because the class was taught a number of times, it became clear to my readers and myself, after reviewing journals when class was over, that the journals, which reflected the students' experiences with racism, had a degree of similarity and predictability. Although their particular experiences with racism would differ, there was certain predictability in the journals. Most students of color would have ongoing, painful, racist experiences and diminished expectations for fairness and justice, and most White students could not sense that there was a problem. So regardless of which students participated in the class, their experiences with race and racism seemed to be quite similar. Finally, because the student voices in this book came from three different classes in three different years, they are more likely to be representative of the experiences of both children of color and White children than a sampling of student voices from only one class or one year.

A final comment about the class. I do not wish our readers to believe that this class is without some tradition in the sociology field. It is a class that is not idiosyncratic. The educational experiences that students had in these classes allowed them to see the world through different lenses and is thus consistent with some of the lessons from the Chicago School of thought (Orcutt, 1996) and the goals of teaching social justice. Just as Chicago was the laboratory for studying society at the turn of the century, we can see how the classroom can provide a laboratory for the study of social issues at the beginning of this century. Whereas the Chicago faculty went into the city to find alternate lenses through which their students could view the world, the diversity and social justice issues represented in many of our large universities can provide the alternative "lenses" that the Chicago faculty were seeking.[3] Thus, it is as agents of social change in our classrooms that we, as educators, teachers, and professors, can provide students with an experience of personal understanding of roles, norms, latent structures, prejudicial beliefs, and racist practices. To take the position that our classrooms are laboratories for studying social justice issues and social problems is intellectually and emotionally more challenging for us as teachers. It is also *a moral position,* for it involves us in the main issues relevant to our democratic society, and it involves students in this same debate. It draws on one of our most important academic and sociological traditions (Illich, 1971; Lynd, 1939; Orcutt, 1996) while also embracing the tenets of education as a form of liberation (Freire, 1973, 1994; McLaren, 1994; Nieto, 1996). My own pedagogy is reflected in the words of Page Smith: "There is no decent, adequate, respectable education, in the proper sense of that much abused word, without personal involvement by a teacher with the needs and concerns, academic and personal, of his/her students" (Smith, 1990). I also believe that university professors have options that they may not be aware of for making the educational experience more meaningful and thus more profoundly touching students' lives. I hope that this book may inspire teachers to accept this challenge.

This book is the result of the efforts of many individuals. I have already mentioned the key teaching done by persons associated with the class: Ruth Alatorre, Dee Gilbert, Ani Karayan, Trang Ming Le, and Jill Stein. I wish to thank and acknowledge the work of Jennifer Nazareno, Donna Garcia, and Rene Emory for preparing the first drafts of the manuscript. Gina Ji Young Kim, Michael Ambriz, and Day Hadaegh prepared the later versions. Theresa Cho, Brandice Reyes, and Shaena Kwok read early versions of the manuscript and provided cogent and substantive editorial comments. Tiffany Chin, Ani Karayan, Trang Minh Le, and Robert Emerson also read the manuscript and posed questions and comments all designed to improve this text. Holly Ann Simonson read a prefinal draft and made editorial and substantive suggestions. Friends who read, commented, and helped include Sherry L. Berkman and Jill Weston. Eric Cheung prepared numerous versions of the manuscript with speed, aplomb, and goodwill. Jill Barker did an excellent job checking references. Karen Datugan typed, edited, and polished the final version of the text.

Michelle Charness, an attorney who specializes in domestic violence prosecution and who recently returned to graduate school to obtain her Ph.D. in Social Welfare at UCLA, came on board and contributed greatly to the focus and clarity of the work through her questions, careful editing, and writing.

Three members of the Kendall Hunt production team were patient, supportive, and facilitated the delivery of the manuscript. Billee Jo Hefel and Michelle Bahr were in charge of overall management of the manuscript and Deb Howes turned my idea of a cover into a wonderful rendering. I thank them all.

Over the years, there have been more than 100 student facilitators who were trained to lead the small-group discussions. The work done by the facilitators on themselves has been especially gratifying to us.

We wish to personally acknowledge the facilitators who supported the goals of the class and who made teaching more exciting and more challenging. They were especially important to the classes we taught. These include: Michael Ambriz, Jennifer Anderson, John Aquino, Hedda Aspacio, Anita Avalos, Brooke Baker, Thomas Barnes, Renata Batarse, Kimberely Berg, Jackie Blanco, Renee Boehm, Ashley Braband, Erron Brumfield, Jason Buccat, Lori Chang, Yara Dahud, Malachi John Davis, Zalika Davis, Poonam Dharni, Andrea Duncan, Tricia Rose Elegino, Devin Elizondo, Erseno Ermo, Donna Estacio, Derrick Evan, Tracey Freed, Rola Ghadban, Marianne Gomis, Tiffany Hamilton, Angie Harris, Doug Hartwell, LaShell Holton, Joyce Hu, Monica Huang, Nicole Josefson, Jennifer Jung, Edit Khachatryan, Hanie Kim, Roger Kim, Karyn Lee, Edna M. Lopez, Becky McConnell, Kenia Mendez, Michelle Mosqueda, Adam Reed, Robert

Romero, Jonathan Rosales, Brandon Rosenthal, Sarah Sandford-Smith, Wesley Sasser, Sheela Wati Sharma, Anna Swanson, Jessica Szegedi, Kelli Tench, Tara Topper, Olga Torres, Sarah Trankiem, Ben Weitz, Ella Vaisberg, Ileana Villalba, Yvette Villalobos, and Amy Wood.

There were 10 seminarians in my education class who carefully read this work prior to its publication and made helpful suggestions. They include: Nerissa Aroonprapun, Jill Ash, Evish Kamrava, Shawn Kang, Jeremy Lalas, Ramiro Mendora, Brandice Reyes, Liz Senguinetti, Elizabeth Serrano, and Chelsea Walsh.

Before this book was published, students in my Honors class "The Social Psychology of Privilege and Oppression" (spring of 2002) read the text in its entirety. Their support and appreciation need to be acknowledged. These include: Angela Aguilar, Jill Barker, Erron Brumfield, Matthew Choi, Edna Cordova, Elizabeth Cruz, Amy Cummings, Lillian Delkhah, Vartan Djihanian, Day Hadaegh, Sophia Henry, Elizabeth Jacobo, Will Kang, Lusine Khachatryan, Nate Lam, Ingrid Larsson, Vi Le, Christina Louie, Jackie Mederos, Elena Paik, Nathalie Polakoff, Blas Romero, Nive Shinde, Michelle Sivert, Carey Holladay Snowden, Kristen Tarjan, Stephanie Toby, Anna Trepetin, Katie Treski, and Lauren White.

As I reread these names just before this book is going off to the printer, for a second edition my goal for a better and more tolerant society is rekindled. So many of these students have gone on to become teachers, lawyers, coaches, parents, political activists, and educators and it is hoped that they will be able to continue to reflect on their own experiences with racism and racist practices to ensure a more just society for all of us.

# INTRODUCTION

# *The Road to Racism*

This book is especially written for the many Americans who may feel that racism in America has lessened. Our research suggests otherwise. In fact, Americans are actually becoming less tolerant of societal diversity. Though many believe that racism is no longer fruitful to discuss, the reader will soon discover how it is a powerful, constant, omnipresent fact of American life. This book is being written at a time when Americans report negative attitudes toward minorities, gays, women, immigrants, and elders (Bobo, 1997; Feagin, 2000; Richardson, Reyes, & Rabow, 1998). Therefore, it seeks to inform those who feel that there is nothing to be discussed, nothing to be understood, or that nothing can be done.[1]

Appreciation of diversity is something that we, as a society, purportedly strive for but have not yet achieved. Widespread lack of understanding, even animosity, between groups is a pressing social and political problem. We live in a climate in which legislators and citizens have voted against affirmative action and elected officials openly campaign for the death penalty for gays (Blumenthal, 1994). Many wish to close our borders and deny basic health care to children. Glass ceilings remain unbroken and there is often no job protection for gay employees (Stewart, 1997). In the year that we began this book, a White male targeted and killed a Black male, shot at Hassidic Jews, and killed a Korean male in Illinois. It was the year in which James Byrd from Texas and Mathew Shepherd from Wisconsin had been murdered, one for being Black and the other for being gay. It was the year in which three synagogues were

---

[1] Today's racism has been posited as symbolic rather than overt (Kinder & Sears, 1981). As the reader will see, the racism described in this text is what Essed (1991) describes. She introduces "everyday racism" as a concept that is "routinely created and reinforced through everyday practices. . . [and] connects structural forces of racism with routine situations in everyday life. It links ideological dimensions of racism with daily attitudes and interprets the reproduction of racism in terms of the experience of it in everyday life" (Essed, 1991). Solorzano (1998) has referred to the everyday experiences of people of color as *microaggressions*.

torched in the state capitol of California. It was the year in which five Jewish children were shot at in Granada Hills, California and one Filipino man, Joseph Ileto, was selected as a "target of opportunity" and then murdered. In the year that we are finishing this book, many urban police departments systematically target African American drivers for the "offense" known as "driving while Black." It is the year in which a major chain of 250 retail clothing stores settled a bias suit in which clerks in these stores had been instructed to closely follow all African American shoppers. It is the year after the presidential vote (Gore vs. Bush, 2000) was radically split along racial lines. And in this same year, all Americans have come to experience racism with the attacks on the World Trade Center and the Pentagon. We are not healed and we are not tolerant. We are deeply, deeply divided (Hacker, 1992). Cries for tolerance, understanding, and pleas for social justice are at a premium. Even the stress placed on political correctness has become repressive, doing little to increase understanding and empathy (Searle, 1993).

In the United States, you can always find someone who will have an opposing opinion and it is of little surprise that some scholars have argued that Americans have become more tolerant (Sniderman & Carmines, 1997; Thernstrom & Thernstrom, 1997; Wolfe, 1998). It is perhaps difficult to reconcile these contradictory views, but Hacker has made one criticism of tolerance. He critiques how some White authors, who believe that racism has diminished, start with the assumption that an "intense dislike of an entire race must pervade the U.S. for racism to exist" (Hacker, 1998). Because intense dislike of any race is not a pervasive phenomenon, many believe that racism is no longer a reality. Of course, we believe that covert and subtle racism is as pernicious as the overt and explicit brand, and in many ways, more dangerous and damaging.[2]

We may not have massive burning of crosses or lynching; the exclusive clubs are out. But racism is not dead. Though James Byrd and Mathew Shepherd may seem like the isolated and random acts of a few "crazies," for many people, these dramatic acts symbolize something more pervasive. There are scholars for whom the deep and pervasive facts of racism and oppression still exist. Professor Beverly Tatum, a psychologist and President of Spelman College, Georgia, (1997) uses a metaphor to illustrate the omnipresence of racism.

---

[2] There have been a number of efforts designed to evaluate Americans' attitudes towards racism. Three important books that have examined attitudes include works by Kinder and Sanders (1996); Schuman, Steeh, Bobo, and Krysan (1997); and Smelser, Wilson, and Mitchell (2001).

I sometimes visualize the ongoing cycle of racism as a moving walkway at the airport. Active racist behavior is equivalent to walking fast on the conveyor belt. The person engaged in active racist behavior has identified with the ideology of White supremacy and is moving with it. Passive racist behavior is equivalent to standing still on the walkway. No overt effort is being made, but the conveyor belt moves the bystanders along to the same destination as those who are actively walking. Some of the bystanders may feel the motion of the conveyor belt, see the active racists ahead of them, and choose to turn around, unwilling to go to the same destination as the White supremacists. But unless they are walking actively in the opposite direction at a speed faster than the conveyor belt—unless they are actively antiracist—they will find themselves carried along with the others.

A social psychologist, Raphael Ezekiel (1995), uses another metaphor to explain the daily doses of racism that we are all exposed to:

Racism is a way of perceiving the world and a way of thinking. To a certain degree, it is part of everyone who lives in a racist society. Imagine growing up next to a cement factory, and imagine the cement dust inevitably becoming a part of your body. As we grow up within a society that is saturated with White racism, year after year we pass through interactions in which White racist conceptions are an unspoken subtext. We make lives in institutions in which this is true. We cannot live from day to day without absorbing a certain amount of White racism into our thoughts. (We similarly absorb homophobia and sexism.) It is foolish to say, "I am not racist." Part of one's mind (if one is White and perhaps if one is a person of color) has necessarily absorbed racist ways of thinking. It is important to discover the subtle ways our culture's racism has affected our thinking: to identify those habits of thought and learn how to keep them from influencing us. We can get tripped up by ideas we don't allow ourselves to acknowledge.

Joe Feagin, a sociologist, (2000), is more specific and concrete about our racial oppression. Feagin is suggesting by implication that we are all racist—we all have racist feelings and we all engage in racist behaviors.

In the United States racism is structured into the rhythms of everyday life. It is lived, concrete, advantageous for Whites, and painful for those who are not White. Even a person's birth and parents are shaped by racism, since mate selection is limited by racist pressures against interracial marriage. Where one lives is often determined by the racist practices of landlords, bankers, and others in the real estate profession. The clothes one wears and what one has to eat are affected by access to resources that varies by position in the racist hierarchy. When one goes off to school, her or his education is shaped by contemporary racism—from the composition of the student body to the character of the curriculum. Where one goes to church is often shaped by racism, and it is likely that racism affects who one's political representatives are. Even getting sick, dying and being buried may be influenced by racism. Every part of the life cycle, and most aspects of one's life, are shaped by the racism that is integral to the foundation of the United States.[3]

## INTRODUCTION TO THE PAINTBRUSH

In this book, we have decided to use a metaphor for illustrating the omnipresent fact of racism in America. The metaphor includes *both* a paintbrush and buckets of white paint. This broad paintbrush moves over and through the lives of children of color in America. The brush is very wide and almost no one can avoid its touch. The brush is always dipped in white paint. Some believe that the paint is benign, but it's not. The paint is corrosive, leaving scars and memories of pain. The white paintbrush is applied differently to children at different ages, and various people do the painting, but the messages are the same. The messages are caustic, critical, and condescending. "Your hair is too curly!" "Your eyes have a weird shape!" "Your eyes are not blue or green and they are ugly!" "You are ugly!" "You have an accent!" "You dress funny!" "Your features are too broad!" "You have a funny name and it is too difficult to pronounce!" "You are dirty!" "You are too dark!" All of these short utterings have a common meaning: "You are not like me, and I don't like you. Since you're not like me, you make me uncomfortable, and because I'm normal and you're not, I'll tell you what I don't like about you." Children of color who are born in the United States and children of color who immigrate to our country are painted and scarred with the strokes of white paint delivered by parents, teachers, friends, and classmates, and by books, magazines, and television. Having been painted so often that it begins to seem normal, children of color finally begin to paint themselves.

The paintbrush is wielded by dominants. When we refer to dominants, we mean a group that has the power to not only differentiate itself from "others" but also the privilege to see its difference as superior. Dominants have a group identity and collective interests. The work they do to maintain their interests often results in prejudice against those who are not members of the dominant group. Dominants and subordinates have existed since the first collectives on earth. Moreover, dominants and subordinates have a relationship to each other (Miller, 1998). The relationship can be as ephemeral and temporary as in playgroups and as permanent as in institu-

---

[3] Feagan, J.R. 2000. Racist America: Roots, current realities, and future reparations. New York. Routledge.

tionalized slavery. The one dominant group that will be discussed in this book is White Americans. There are certainly other dominants such as males, heterosexuals, able-bodied people, and Christians.[4] Whites are the people who, through no fault or effort of their own, belong to the normative race. Whiteness frequently brings unearned privilege and advantages (McIntosh, 1998). Some White people understand how Whiteness brings privilege, but many White people are often unable to see these advantages. This White privilege is the flip side of racism (Rothenberg, 1998a). Because dominants are the standard, they do not know their subordinates well. They don't have to. They need only look to themselves to see who they should be and what they need to know. Most White people, when they look at themselves, don't see race and racism. How can they? Their race is normal and racism is not part of their world. It need not be noticed. Subordinates, on the other hand, know dominants very well. They notice them immediately because their survival, achievement, and accomplishments often depend on dominant recognition. Subordinates cannot avoid hearing the evaluations from Whites. Whites evaluate the differences to subordinates as something that is "less." Subordinates cannot escape dominants' messages. In America, the message comes directly and indirectly from many sources. Subordinates get the message until they often begin to internalize the view of themselves seen by dominants. Dominants are not born with brush in hand, but at a young age they acquire one and quickly learn how to use it. There is much to be learned. The brush is made up of stereotypes, prejudices, philosophies, beliefs, and ideas in which "White" and all of the features, qualities, beliefs, values, and norms that go with it are the standard against which all others are judged. Dominants use the brush to paint those who do not meet these standards, and thus a series of interpersonal and personal dynamics is put into motion with painful consequences. The political and social consequences of these acts are the perpetuation of racism.

Dominants, the wielders of the brush, learn a philosophy about their rightful place in the world. Many dominants exert great effort to justify their prejudices, which in turn supports their interests and goals. Much of the history of dominants in the United States is extremely malevolent. It is a history of poisoning and discarding cultures and peoples because they were perceived as different and thus dangerous (Takaki, 1993, 1998). However, though those histories need to be told and remembered, this book is not about those stories. Instead, it is a book about today's racism

---

[4]A survey of efforts in higher education to increase diversity has been made by Hurtado, Milem, Clayton-Pederson, and Allen (1999). A survey of the views of White students on affirmative action has been completed by Chesler and Peet (2002).

and prejudice, the legacy of those histories. It is a book about the more invidious and subtle sides to racism revealed by our students. It is racism in which "God Bless You" and "Have a Nice Day" are prefaced by a refusal to rent an apartment or to accept a check. There is a legacy of racism that exists and is enacted daily in the United States and it touches all our lives. Racism is a daily fact of life in our families, schools, playgrounds, corporations, smaller businesses, and universities. Though many dominants do not intentionally discriminate and do not mean to be prejudiced, the white paintbrush creates a world in which dominants and the traits and features that they possess are the standard by which all others are evaluated. Those who are different are painted as deviant and somehow inferior. These prejudices are used as justification for exploitation but much of the power of the brush lies not in its use as a deliberate weapon of domination, but rather in much subtler uses as a marker of what is "normal" and right.

Dominants learn at an early age that people of color are different. They learn that these "different" people must prove themselves in order to be seen as good and "normal." Often, they learn that subordinates are not worth knowing at all. Indeed, subordinates are often not even seen or noticed. When subordinates *are* noticed, they may be seen as esoteric, strange, overemotional, funny, lazy, stupid, sick, dangerous, or un-American. Further, dominants do not learn about subordinates from subordinates themselves, but rather from other dominants. Specifically, dominants are instructed about their exclusivity by their parents, friends, classmates, books, magazines, and television. They learn to teach themselves and each other.

To practice dominance, dominants use the brush to seek out difference and to ensure that subordinates learn about themselves from the perspective of the powerful. Because dominants have power, they can use the paintbrush to make all kinds of strokes. The brush wielders can label groups as inferior. They can suggest and command social roles appropriate for subordinates.

The paintbrush is wielded when dominants can benefit economically, politically, and socially by exploiting their difference and using their power to paint subordinates as undeserving, unmotivated, less rational, less civilized, less intelligent, dangerous, and even subhuman. A prime example of this is American slavery. Other examples are what dominants did to Native Americans, Chinese laborers, and to Japanese Americans during World War II. This domination and painting of the other as "less" occurred with all the European efforts of colonization, the missions established in North, Central, and South America, and in the *Bracero* program developed by our government to import and exploit migrant Mexican workers. We exclusively focus on race and racism, but we wish to remind the reader that race is only one pattern of domination and subordination. It is this same pattern of domination that can be observed today as corporations deny benefits to homosexual partners because their unions are deemed "unnatural." It happens every time a woman is denied a leadership position because she might be "too emotional" to handle the pressure. It occurs in every collective in which there is an uneven distribution of power.

Prisons, universities, corporations, and families are all collectives in which dominants have views about what is right and fair. Not surprisingly, these views are usually at odds with many of the views of subordinates. For the readers who feel that they have never been dominant, think about your younger siblings or cousins. Think about your view of them—their faults, their lesser value, and their lesser worth. For readers who feel they have never been a subordinate, think about your parents and the ways in which they have found fault with you and sought to criticize and correct your behavior—behavior that in your view was completely justifiable and responsible.

Dominant groups have their paintbrushes ready to provide and impose morality, philosophy, standards of beauty, and even scientific "truths" that justify their own and subordinates' rightful places and positions in the world. When parents (dominants) and children (subordinates) are involved, we assume the inequalities will be somewhat temporary. Under temporary inequality, differences can enhance each party. Children can gain wisdom and guidance. Parents can learn patience and acceptance. As we shall see, the inequality between Whites in the United States as dominants and people of color in the United States as subordinates tends to be an almost permanent inequality in our country. Here, differences do not enhance or enrich but rather diminish each party.

In the United States, as we begin a new millennium, wielders of the paintbrush often believe they are supporting equality. Most Americans don't believe in slavery and do not believe they are racists. Most dominants do not believe that they possess a paintbrush. Those who do know about the brush are likely to believe that the strokes delivered by themselves and others are harmless or even helpful. Dominants often refuse to accept the relevance and reality that race has for subordinates. Yet, for subordinates, race as Cose said, ". . . is the only relevant factor defining their existence" (Cose 1993, p. 28).

In this book, the reader will see how race is a salient fact of life for college students of color. Although we have no slave owners or internment camps, and though slave wages have been replaced by minimum wages, anti-Black, anti-Asian, anti-immigrant, anti-Middle Eastern, anti-Semitic, anti-Latin and anti-gay remarks are often acceptable. The reader will see that the brush strokes delivered by dominants do not come from members of the Klan, skinheads, or Aryan groups. Peers, teachers, parents, and professors deliver them. They are delivered by people who believe in fairness, in God, and in the United States. They are people who go to church and temple, and they pay their taxes. They are honest people—but they are racists. They are delivered by you and I, by all of us. And they are not harmless. They are delivered by dominants to subordinates and from subordinates to other subordinates as well as dominants. The latter form of racism, though painful and important, lacks the power that accompanies the racism from dominance. The painting does not promote equality, fairness, or justice. The brush strokes do not enrich the differences between us. As they scar and hurt individuals, they also undermine the sense of justice and fairness that Americans believe should be their right.[5]

This book is about college students at an elite, highly diverse, public university, who struggled to acknowledge and then confront their own racism, stereotypes, and prejudices. Most of the students were raised in California and one might assume that these students would have been exposed to and learned to appreciate diversity, as California has one of the most diverse populations in the entire world. And, indeed, no race or ethnic group constitutes a majority in the state of California. But racism seems to be the experience of almost every single student we have ever known; it is in the hearts and minds of college students. In other words, the students at this university have been unable to find "fresh air;" many breathe in the dust of racism without necessarily being conscious of it. For others who are aware of the dust and poison, it is a daily attack on their health, well-being, and worth. "The conveyor belt continues to run." Racism and prejudice are alive and flourishing. These UCLA students experienced prejudice, racism, anti-Semitism, sexism, and homophobia. Its extent and pervasiveness can be debated, but it must be called what it is—in most cases it was ignorance and in other cases it was and is evil. This racism touches all of us every day of our lives and in every institution of our country. But, though the students you will hear from have known enormous hurt and pain, many still had hope and were able to move beyond their scars to a place of forgiveness and transcendence. Though they were our students, they are your brothers, your sisters, your cousins, your neighbors, your fellow citizens, and your children. We must not continue to fail them.

# I

# *Introducing the Paintbrush:*
## *Learning to Paint from Family and Peers*

How do dominants learn to paint? From where does the desire or even the need to paint arise? Infants are not born with the desire to paint. Instead, infants and toddlers treat each other with equality regardless of race. Indeed, early childhood may be the only time in all of our lives that we are truly colorblind. However, at some point things change and children of all colors begin to learn to paint. Children learn to paint by participating in a cultural system, which provides them with categories for classifying objects and people. All societies or groups within societies determine which differences are important for distinguishing one group from another. In the United States, a person's skin color is a marker for categorizing people because it is considered to be important. By the age of 7, 90% of children are aware of racial categories. They have begun to act like the adults of their culture (Hirschfeld, 1996).

In these first two chapters we will show how children learn to use the paintbrush. We will show how well-meaning people learn to act as racists. After reviewing the students' journals it becomes clear that children learn to paint from many sources. These include family members, peer groups, and others in society such as the media, teachers and classmates in school, law enforcement officials, and persons in the workforce.

This first chapter will show the reader how children and young adults learn to paint from their families and peers. This chapter will also reveal how minority children learn to paint themselves. In Chapter 2, we will demonstrate how the other major institutions in society provide painting lessons.

## I. LEARNING TO PAINT FROM ONE'S FAMILY

We learn many things from our family members. They often teach us about who we are by seeking to instill their own religious beliefs. They help shape and formulate our interests, our values, our goals, and our very connection to each other and the world around us. Additionally, they instruct us about shame, guilt, oppression, hate, and racism. Because children are so impressionable and the adults in their lives are so important, it is our contention that racism is learned in the bosom of the family. As such, this learning is very powerful for it provides the canvas for future painting lessons. Although instructions in painting will continue as children grow, we believe that family is the key influence for and against racism. Specifically, family members can instill the belief that being White is synonymous with privilege and therefore entitles one to paint. A family member can actually give a young child the paintbrush with the instruction, in fact, the duty, to paint all that is different. In this first excerpt, a White female describes her father's attempt to teach her the strokes of racism.

> I was a junior in high school and I had a friend who was Black. I never paid any attention to this fact but as soon as he started to like me I found out something about my father that I didn't like. The boy's name was M and he called me one day. My dad answered the phone and gave it to me. I talked to him for about 20 minutes and when I got off the phone my father started asking me who he was. I told him because I thought he was just being a protective father. When I described him as being Black, I thought my dad was going to faint. He had this weird look on his face and it scared me. I thought I had done something wrong but I couldn't understand what it was. He told me that he didn't think it was a good idea for him to continue calling and he told me he didn't want me to hang out with him anymore. I was very confused and upset. I asked my mom why he said this to me and she explained that he didn't believe in interracial relationships. (White, female)

The next example details how a White, nontraditional student, growing up in the South, gets a painting lesson in racism. She describes how she had to "learn her place." This is similar to Richard Wright's explanation of how he had to learn his place in the South (Wright, 2001). He had to learn how he must hold his head down when coming upon a White person, how he must walk off the sidewalk to let a White person pass, how he could not stare or look at White women, and how he had to speak to White people. Our student grew up in the South in the 1950s prior to the civil rights movement. Her place was based on privilege and domination, the opposite side of racism.

> When I was a little girl, my mother used to take me with her every summer to visit her family in the South. Cooking was tantamount to a religious observance, we always had homemade biscuits for breakfast, everyone spoke with long drawly accents, and everything was completely and totally segregated. Blacks went to one school and Whites to another and not one restaurant in town served "coloreds." When my cousins and I went to the movies on Saturday afternoons, we entered the theater through the "Whites

Only" entrance. When we were thirsty, we drank from the "Whites Only" fountain. When we were tired and needed a place to sit down, we sat in the "Whites Only" section of the railroad station. Blacks, who were "coloreds" in polite conversation and "nigras" in private, were forced to use facilities that had signs above them reading "Colored Only." Their signs were not as nice as ours. When I walked down Main Street with my Grandpa in the afternoons, any Black man walking towards us was obliged to step off the curb and into the street so that we could keep walking without having to endure the whiff of "coloreds in the air."

I can't say that the segregation I experienced bothered me as an act of evil in and of itself. I do know that I especially liked E, my Granny's Black maid, and would always ask to ride along when my mother or one of my aunts "carried" her home for the weekend. She lived in the bottoms, an area with dark red soil on the edge of the piney woods near Lake Texas. There were lots of farms in the bottoms. Black people didn't have farms; they lived near them because most of the Blacks lived on land that was carved from a larger White-owned property and given to them after the Civil War. Some of the Black people who lived in the bottoms had mothers or fathers who were slaves that were owned by the parents or grandparents of the White farmers that still lived there.

E's house was a shack really, a tumbledown collection of old, unpainted wood, with a small porch out front. Whenever we drove up in front of E's house, the car was always surrounded by a group of five or six Black kids about my age and I knew that they were impressed with the car we were driving. They always ran up to us from behind the shack in a big giggly lump. They always looked like they were having so much fun that I wished that I could run with them. They peered in the windows of the car as though we were a sideshow curiosity and I remember wondering what it would be like to be standing on the outside of the car looking in. We were special, I knew that much, and it embarrassed me to no end. I remember seeing E's husband who had lost one of his legs in World War II, sitting on the porch waiting for his wife to arrive. I wondered how he got around when she wasn't there.

One day I rode along as Aunt P made the end-of-the-week run to E's house. I sat turned around in the front seat of the car. I was 8 years old and E and I were having a lively conversation. I asked E if I could come into her house when we got there and she said that I sure could. When we pulled up to the front of her house, I jumped out of the car and started to run up the path to E's front porch. Her husband was sitting there and he smiled at me. Just as quick, I felt my Aunt P's hand on my upper arm, snatching me back to the car. I protested that E said I could come in and my aunt didn't say a word. She threw me in the front seat, closed my door, got into the driver's side and we drove off. After about 30 seconds of shaking her head in silence, she said, "Child, you have got to learn your place." (White, female)

The South is not the only place in America where painting instructions are given. In the following example, a White male visiting the Midwest describes his grandfather's instructions.

> I visited my grandparents in the Midwest when I was in the third grade and gained exposure to explicit racism. My grandpa referred to an African American as a "jigaboo," one of the first times I can remember hearing a derogatory name for a minority. I heard this term before, but I had never heard "nigger" used. I respected my grandpa and therefore did not question his racial views. Hearing my grandpa talk to me about "jigaboos" and how they were not welcome in his house gave me my first notion on White superiority . . . I had been attending a Christian church since I was a baby and considered myself a moral person. I knew that I should be a moral person, but also had been implanted with the conflicting notion that Whites are superior. I wanted to treat all humans with compassion yet my grandpa was a respectable man . . . how could I look badly upon his views? I was in a racial dilemma. I had realized that people look different and I didn't know how to act upon this fact. I played with many friends of racial minorities at school but never questioned what my grandpa told me. (White, male)

A White female who grew up in the Northwest describes her grandmother's racist beliefs and teachings.

> As for racism, I have never had much experience with it other than from my family. My grandma is very racist. She lives in Oregon and when we go to visit her, I sometimes feel uncomfortable. She still refers to African Americans as "niggers" and I feel that this word is wrong. Maybe I even feel it is dirty. I never use that word and don't even like to repeat it. She is very forward and believes in the "Southern Ways." That is, in the South, most people are very racial. They do not believe that they are equals to African Americans. They believe that they are superior to them. My grandma still carries on the stereotype of "slave boy." I hate it when she talks that way but I could never disrespect her by telling her she is wrong. I just quiver inside and try to ignore it. (White, female)

A White male, growing up in the Northeast, recalls lessons learned from his parents when he was 12 years old. The message is clear: being White means being "good." People of color don't behave well, he is told, and when his conduct is less than exemplary, he is "no better than them."

> The summer before I was to enter the seventh grade, we moved from our racially mixed neighborhood. Up until then, I had gone to school with African Americans, Puerto Ricans, Native Americans, and Asians. I had a hard time making friends at my new school. Everyone was White. I was the new kid and I got picked on a lot. As a teenager, I fell in with a gang and got into some trouble. I remember sitting in the driveway in my Dad's car with him one time when he was really angry at me. He said, "Jesus

Christ! What's the matter with you? Don't you know how hard your mother and I have had to work to get you kids out of the old neighborhood, away from the niggers and spics? And still, you're no better than them, for Christ's sake!" (White, male)

A White woman analyzes the origins of her racism towards Asians. The student describes the paintbrush her mother gave her. The brush would be used to paint Asians as cheap and less deserving of equal treatment.

When I think about where some of my racism toward Asians could have started, I recall the things my parents taught me in regards to "Orientals," as they were called in those days. My parents owned a business that I often worked in to secure spending money. When an Asian would walk in, my mother would make derogatory remarks about how "tight" they were (with money) and how they were notorious for asking for discounts. She therefore did not greet or treat them in the same manner as other customers. She would be more apt to ignore them and try to avoid spending too much time with them. This left a lasting impression on me, and I began to make similar attributions when working at the shop. The stereotype became internalized. (White, female)

In a telling example of cross-generation racism, a White female describes how she learned to view African Americans through the teachings of various painters in her family. She recalls that her grandfather and father were the main instructors of racism.

When I first learned about race I see the innocent little girl I once was who was so unaffected by racism or divisions and I wish I could be her now. All her stereotypes I've inadvertently picked up, internalized, all the racism covering over my once pure heart. When I was a little older I remember my grandparents espousing racial epithets and phrases like, "Why would you want to watch a show with a bunch of niggers in it?" when referring to the TV show "The Jeffersons." Or they would say things like, "Look at all those Blacks on TV now." Saying this in front of a child is so inappropriate; it makes me so angry now that I didn't fight back more. I'd say something to the effect of, "Oh grandpa, that is not nice or that is stupid and racist." . . . I was about 12 or 13 [at the time]. My father would say a lot of things about Black people being lazy and not wanting to work, therefore, he wasn't going to support them. (White, female)

Another female, White student recalls learning about racism at the young age of 6 from family members. Specifically, her father and brothers instructed her that she was not to socialize with an African American boy in her class.

I was 6 years old and there was a little Black boy in my class whom I adored; I had my first crush on him. I told some people on the bus on the way home one day after he had gotten off and they made fun of me for it. I don't recall who made fun of me but I remember my older brothers telling me that I couldn't like a Black boy, as if something was wrong with me. I remember being confused and feeling a sense of shame. At that point it dawned on me that something must be wrong with me for liking him. I don't recall what if or what my parents said, if anything, although later my father made his thought on the matter clear. He would not approve of my ever dating, much less marrying, a Black man. Since growing older I've challenged him on these thoughts and his rationalization now is that the world is a hard enough place without being in a biracial relationship and if we had kids how difficult that would be for them. Of course, I don't buy his bigoted excuses and we have had many heated debates about these issues. (White, female)

Though one might hope that all minorities who have been victims of racism would unite to fight against it, this is not always the case. Unfortunately, among these students, the joining of different minorities to end racism against other minority groups is rare. Instead, the suppression of one race seems to lead to the desire to squelch another; it's as if each group needs to assert its position of dominance on the hierarchical ladder, which is achieved through labeling and stigmatizing anyone who is different. Why would minorities hurt or have prejudice against other minorities? Growing up in the United States means we are all painters. No one escapes. Minorities also breathe the air of racism. We all play in the buckets of White racist paint. When we emerge from the bucket we all know how to paint. So it is not surprising that minorities treat other people of color the same way that dominants treat them. However, a major difference between dominant versus subordinate racism is power. When dominants treat subordinates as lesser, there usually are norms and traditions to enforce the difference. When subordinates treat other subordinates as lesser, there is relatively no institutional power to enforce that difference. Therefore, the power of dominants is more critical to the maintenance of racism than subordinate to subordinate racism.

In the next three examples, children of color reveal the instructions in painting from their families. Sometimes the instructions direct the child to paint particular minority groups. A Chicana recalls the racist views her father instilled in her regarding African Americans. Her father actually taught her to fear African American males simply based on their color. The phenomenon of subordinate racism against other subordinates cannot be ignored.

I can honestly reveal that depending on how a Black man "looks" I fear them. I know this is racist but the more I think about, actually I fear any man that has a certain "look." I know that it is not a whole race of people that does wrong, it is that person as an individual. It is unfair and detrimental to classify and damn their whole race for what one person has done.

And I am conscious that sometimes I think this way. I learned at home how to be a racist because my father always had this deep hatred for anyone other than Mexican. He had a sinister loathing for Blacks. I was told to never have Black friends and to stay away from them because, according to him, they were inherently evil and lazy and would get me in trouble. An early childhood experience with a Black woman who befriended me caused my father to be physically violent. He beat me for associating with her. This was when I was in preschool, and incidentally was the catalyst in reinforcing his views onto me. (Chicana, female)

Similarly, an Indian American female recounts how she came to have racist feelings towards Asians. Specifically, she remembers her mother painting all Asians as the same or under the generic category of Orientals.[1] When this student corrects her mother's use of this derogatory term, her mother quickly repeats it. In other words, the painter was not willing to acknowledge her daughter's attempt to change the canvas.

My racist attitudes about Asians come from my home. My mother always calls Asians "Orientals." I just found out, last year, that this is not the correct term. Oriental is used for furniture and food, not people. When I told this to my mother, she said "oh" and did not think twice when she called them Oriental again. I do not know if she forgot or if she is overlooking them as people with feelings. I also began to realize how I am sometimes like my mother. I often ask people of color questions like "Where are you from?" and when they answer "San Diego," I ask again. In this class, I realized that the girl is from San Diego and not from Korea because she was not born there. Up to this point, I never really realized what an idiotic question I was asking and what an idiot I looked to others I interacted with. Even worse, I realized how many people I must have offended with questions such as these. (Indian American, female)

In the following excerpt, a Filipino male describes the powerful influence that his father had upon him. His father taught him to be suspicious of Filipinos.

Throughout high school, I often painted myself as "White" and not Asian to be accepted in my White peer group and to make myself an "exception" to "normal" Filipinos. I often made a big deal out of my racial make-up, highlighting the fact that I was "7/8 Filipino and 1/8 White because my great-grandfather was White." Often I also argued that I was literally "White inside" in order to distance myself from Filipinos and to assimilate

---

[1] Beginning in the late 1960s and early 1970s, Asian American activists rejected the term "Oriental" because it "connotes images of the passive, the exotic, and the foreign" (Lee, 1996, p. 44). The label "Oriental" makes it easier for the Western mind to treat Asians like the "other." See Said's (1978) book *Orientalism*.

into the White culture. Because of my good grades, I felt that I had more in common with the honors students, who in my community were predominantly White. Because of "high academic status," I looked down (elitism) on "stupid-gangsta Filipinos" who wore baggy pants—a blanket and narrow view of them as a group.

I participated in racial jokes that specifically ridiculed the Asians in order to disconnect myself from the gangster Filipinos. Where did all of this self-distancing come from? I think that I learned to feel "different" and "special" because of my father. As a young child, he often warned me to be suspicious of Filipinos because he said they were like crabs: if one were to succeed and make it out of the bucket (my father), the others would enviously pull him down. Though he has many friends, he makes sure that we remember that they weren't educated like him. (Filipino, male)

Not all children accept parental instruction. In this next excerpt, White parents instruct their 8-year old son to have nothing to do with his classmate. The parents are very explicit about why their White son should not play and hang out with an Asian female student.

When I was around the third grade, 8 years old, I started to have a crush on a boy in my class. He was my best friend. He was a handsome, tall, big brown-eyed and light brown-haired boy. He looked nothing like the boys I grew up with in my home country. He reminded me of my favorite actor, John Travolta. We would play with each other every day. We played tetherball, we ran around the school playing tag, and we often studied together. We spend most of our time during the lunch hours. I started to like him so much so I decided to tell him. That afternoon, after school, I called him to ask him about homework assignment. I then said bluntly, "I like you!" He paused and laughed and played it off. It hurt so much because it was actually my first time I had liked a boy. The next day, I was determined that I was going to ask him if he wanted to be my boyfriend. His answer to my question was so sharp and it felt like a knife had rammed into my heart. He said, "I just like you as a friend. You're funny, but you're not my type." TYPE? We were 8 years old!!! I asked him why and he said, "I like girls like me." I could not understand him. He then said, "My parents told me that I shouldn't hang out with you too much because you're not like us. You're different. You don't look like me. See? I have big eyes and my skin is lighter." I was so enraged. His parents, including him, were prejudging me strictly on my appearance. They wanted me to be like them. He told me that if I had bigger eyes and I had lighter skin, that he would like me. He said, "maybe my parents will let you be my friend if you had made your skin Whiter and your hair lighter." The next day after school, I went home and tried to rub my skin off with a towel. I felt so ridiculous and stupid. But I guess I must have really liked him because no matter how much I knew this would not help, I was still trying my hardest to make my skin lighter. (Asian, female)

Families can provide painting lessons, which may be continued from one generation to the next. Occasionally, the instructions can be ignored or rejected. Sometimes parents provide less-direct instructions in painting. They may be unable or unwilling to openly discuss racial issues with their children. Consider this example taken from my class discussion. A Black student recalls overhearing a White mother explaining race to her child. The child asked, "Mommy, why is that man so dark?" The mother responded "God probably decided to leave him in the oven a little bit longer but we shouldn't make him feel bad." After my student reported the story to his classmates, two other students of color also indicated that they had heard similar comments from White parents to their children. This response from a parent is not idiosyncratic. Helms (1992) cites this exact example and describes a number of other comments that children make to parents "Mommy, look at the chocolate man. Can I bite him?" or "Why is that man so dirty?" Many parents are embarrassed by a child's innocent questions. The embarrassment encourages children to feel the same discomfort that their parents feel. Children learn that color is a "handicap." Children learn that being White is better, and even favored by God. Children learn that race is a sensitive issue that makes many adults uncomfortable and they should not talk about it.

Most adults teach their children to paint other children and adults of color. Unfortunately, most adults do not have the understanding of how to talk to their children about race. Professor Beverly Tatum illustrates how she insightfully handled a comment about difference made by her son. She had set some eggs out on the kitchen counter. Some of the eggs were brown and some of the eggs were White. Her son commented on the fact that the eggs were not all the same color. "Yes," she said, "they do have different shells. But look at this!" She cracked open a white egg. "See, they are different on the outside, but the same on the inside. People are the same way. They look different on the outside, but they are the same on the inside" (Tatum, 1997). Though some families do teach their children to understand, welcome, or appreciate skin difference, such teachings are rare.

## II. LEARNING TO PAINT FROM ONE'S PEER GROUP

Family members are not the only teachers of racism. Though the family plants the seed of racism, our students seemed to learn more stereotypes and hate from their peers than any other group of painters. The peer group teaches its applicant the rules for participation and full acceptance. Therefore, it is not surprising that many of the students reported learning racial stereotypes and prejudices from their social cliques. Moreover, the peer group's teaching of racism was often achieved through a combination of both subtle and explicit messages.

Like the family, the peer group is a breeding ground that instills the superiority of one group over another. The peer group empowers its own members who perpetuate the values of the group and reward those who are loyal. This goal must be accomplished for the peer group to successfully exist, and is often achieved at the expense of others. Both White and non-White children learn to label and ostracize the other in the confines of their own social group.

A 6-year-old Korean child learns about her deficiencies from her White peers. They first treat her like a "China doll" and then they give her specific instructions about what she would have to do to belong to their peer group. They suggest that she needs to change her skin color and hair color. They even seem to believe that the shape of their eyes allows them to see more clearly.

> I had just come to the United States and the first school I had attended had very few students of color. My brother and I made up the only two Asians in the school; there was one African American, and one Hispanic. This was San Dimas, CA in 1982. The first set of friends I had were White girls from middle-class families. We were only 6 years old and though I did not understand them, we communicated using our hand motions and our facial gestures. They would talk amongst themselves, but I did not understand. It took me about 6 months to fully understand the English language. Though my pronunciations were not perfect, I understood most all of the language used by my peers. The girls would approach me and touch my hair and feel my skin and make facial gestures. They looked confused and looked in awe. They would say, "you have darker skin than us, you have such dark, straight hair, and you have such small eyes." They looked astonished, like I was some antique China doll. They were confused at what they were seeing. They did not know how to respond to my features, and I did not know how to respond to their words. They would also ask me, "Do you take showers, do you see clearly through those eyes of yours, and does your hair wash out from that color?" They would also say, "When you go home today, try to scrape it off, maybe it will come off, and maybe if you wash your hair, it wouldn't be so dark."
>
> They were so cruel even though I believe they did not mean to be. I ran into the restroom and looked at myself in the mirror. I was darker, I had black hair, and my eyes were half the size of theirs. They would often say "Chinese, Japanese, Cantonese," while they were squinting their eyes with their fingers.
>
> I went home that day and watched an episode of the Brady Bunch on television. I saw that Jan Brady put lemons on her face to get rid of freckles. I ran to my mother and asked for lemons. She thought I wanted to make lemonade, so we went to the store and I bought a bag of lemons. The mo-

ment I got home, I ran into the restroom and locked myself in. I could not imagine the reaction from my mother if she had known what I was doing. I started to get scared and nervous. I quickly peeled all of the lemons using a plastic knife and started applying it onto my skin and hair. I thought this would make me lighter and make my hair lighter as well.

The next morning when I woke up from bed, I ran straight to the mirror. Unfortunately, I found the same person I had seen the day before. I saw the dark skin, the dark hair and the slanted eyes. For weeks, I had irritated skin. I was miserable. I was not only dark but scratching myself everywhere. However, through all this, I was the best smelling kid in the whole class. (Korean, female)

In the next example, a Filipino male describes how his participation with his peers would mean belittling others.

I am very ashamed to talk about it now, but my friends and I used to come up with names for people. We had this inside joke of speaking backwards, so that no one else would understand. I can't believe we used to do this, but whenever we would see an Asian that was really "Fresh off the Boat" or newly immigrated we would call him or her a "kcajed pin" which meant, in a roundabout way, "jacked nip." (Filipino, male)

Another Filipino male analyzes his negative views towards Latinos. This student, in part, attributes his racism to hearing his peer group's derogatory stereotypes about Latinos as dirty and uneducated. These early stereotypes influenced his view of Mexican students and his belief that they were only admitted because of affirmative action.

It is hard for me to admit this, and I feel shitty for thinking this way, but prior to taking this class I used to look at some Mexicans and say they got in here because of affirmative action. But from this class, I can honestly say that I am looking at people now on a personal level. I used to believe that I could figure out a person just by knowing their ethnicity. It's funny, but this very act that I did, I hate in other people when they do it to me. My friends in Napa forced their negative views of Mexican onto me. Mexicans were the field workers who picked the grapes. They were looked upon as uneducated and dirty. What changed my views was my self-realization. The hatred I felt so long while growing up and being looked upon as different, I was in turn doing it to another ethnicity. So now I try to look at everyone equally and unbiased. (Filipino, male)

This student also acknowledges that some of his racism towards Latinos actually arises from the prejudices and discrimination he suffered growing up as a minority himself. He implicitly recognized that by stigmatizing another minority group, he somehow felt empowered or less different. This student was able to begin to question the prejudicial practices of his peer group and to decide for himself that he did not align with their message of hate.

In terms of the collegiate experience, there are few peer groups that maintain the type of powerful hold on shaping the ideals of the students more than the Greek system. Though minority groups have their own fraternities and sororities, the Greek system tends to remain an exclusive club of White privilege. As exclusive clubs, they are potential breeding grounds for prejudice and oppression. Indeed, within the confines of some fraternity and sorority houses lies shockingly raw racism. In this first example, a White male describes the ongoing, omnipresent racism in his fraternity.

> I had asked why his fish tank was so dirty, and his roommate replied to me by saying, "Oh don't worry, I'm probably going to have some Mexican come and clean it up. It will be funny to watch, and I won't even pay him much." Two minutes later, I heard one of S's friends call him a "Jew bastard" for not sharing his dessert with him. I could not believe my ears. Possibly the worst thing about the whole situation was the fact that there was one Latino male in the whole house and he heard what these guys were saying. He didn't say a word, but he definitely wasn't laughing. This type of shit happens all the time. The fraternity single-handedly slammed almost every single race there was except their own. I heard "smelly nip," "lazy porch monkey," and even "wetback," in the short time I was there. (White, male)

In this second example a White female has been afraid to disclose the fact that she is in a sorority house. She is ashamed of the practices of her house and the entire Greek system, which she knows to support privilege and exclusivity. She would like to confront what she sees and hates about racism, but she is also afraid of losing her privileges.

> For the past 5 weeks, I have basically hidden the fact that I'm a part of the Greek system. Well, I am more than a part of it, I hold a high position in my house. The fact that I have hidden this part of my identity says quite a bit. It shames me to be part of this discriminating organization in mixed company (yet another manifestation of my dominant mentality—ignoring the problem; it's not real if you don't talk about it). As much as I've tried to defend and prove that my house is different, I have found it harder and harder to do so. There is only one black sorority member in the entire system and a handful of Latinas. Although there are quite a few Asians, as a whole, Panhellenic (comprised of sororities with houses) is around 80–90% White. Yet, as much as I am disturbed by our various practices and exclusive membership, I cannot imagine deactivating (which leaves me with a heavy sense of guilt that I cover up by believing anyone could join though I know in my heart it's not true). My feelings about belonging to this organization are very much tied to my feelings about being White. Both of these facets of my identity have undeniable advantages, which I am afraid to lose; they have become a part of my life. It terrifies me that I would probably be miserable if I woke up tomorrow without these advantages. It seems to be a complex situation—individually, I win

because I gain an edge and maintain it, yet morally, I lose as I perpetuate and propagate what I hate about this world. (White, female)

Painting is not restricted to dominants painting subordinates. Subordinates can sometimes paint their fellow subordinates when behavior challenges the peer groups' norms. An African American male describes the tension that can be set in motion when one acts against the beliefs of the peer group. This student stepped outside the boundaries of his clique when he dated a White girl. Specifically, this student recalls how he learned to stand up for what he believed in even if his peers disapproved.

I dated a White girl in high school, and although none of the Black women at school wanted to date me, they were very upset that I was dating a White girl. They constantly made racial comments about she and I, and even went to my younger sister (who was in the ninth grade) and talked poorly about me to her. After speaking with my father about dating someone out of my own race, he reminded me that in God's eyes, everyone is the same color. Soon after, I decided that I did not have to be Black enough for them. I just had to be myself and stand up for what I believed in. (African American, male)

In another example of subordinates being painted by other subordinates, an Asian female remembers how her own Asian peer group shunned her when she went to a dance with a White boy. She eventually learns to move beyond the anger and shame she felt from the label "White washed" imposed by her peers.

I cannot relate to some Asians who feel that they can only relate to other Asians. I feel like those people are closed minded and have a false sense of pride in their Asian heritage. Many of them don't know the first thing about the native land or culture. As a freshman in high school, I went to a dance with a White guy and since that day, the label "White washed" stuck on me, no matter how many Asian friends I hung out with. I struggled with this label, feeling anger, shame, disgust. Then I got over it. I thought, what do they know about me? I gained enough confidence to look past it and even not to hate the labelers. (Asian, female)

In the following example, a Filipina woman describes the conflict she endures when she refuses to accept the prejudice that she overhears. She fights against the stereotypes her own peer group maintains for Persian people.

I can recall playing the role of the ally when I was with a friend one time and we were just talking in the Kerckhoff patio. Now in that patio, most of the people there are Persian. I guess they just tend to congregate there. Well, my friend proceeds to tell me the same things or "complaints" I've heard many people say before and after about Persians. They're too loud, obnoxious, and [question] why do they always have to sit in the patio? People at my work at the Kerckhoff Coffeehouse always complain about them. To me, sometimes they get on my nerves because they can be really obnoxious, but I try not to play it up or else I'll be just like my friends and people at work and I don't want to be. So, my point is that I think it's really kind of jacked how so many people complain about them. Also, now people think that just because I always defend the people they make fun of or complain about, that I am calling them racist or that I'm just some uptight person who can never hear or listen or be exposed to anything remotely bad. That, actually, is tough to deal with. (Filipina, female)

The power of the peer group is captured in the above excerpt. This student has rebelled against the stereotypes her friends inflict on Persian people. However, her courage to fight racism is not met with open arms. Instead, as she asserts, she is criticized for speaking out against the group's collective mindset.

Some readers might believe that on the sports fields and gyms of America, the playing fields are level. However, the following excerpts suggest the powerful privilege that White males can exert on our "level playing field." In this excerpt, a White student admits his own resentment and discomfort about his behavior when a subordinate had the talent and audacity to out perform his peer painters. In recalling this experience, the student was prompted to reflect and examine his racism. He struggles to understand why he let his peers continually foul a Black teammate.

It's now 3 weeks into the course and I remember a distant high school memory. When he arrived on campus he was about 115 lbs and 5'7 inches. He was a small kid, but he could play some serious basketball. From the first day of practice, I knew, aside from his exemplary basketball skills, that he would stand out from within and from without. First of all, he is a freshman and a tiny one at that. Second of all, he dressed completely different from the rest of us. To add to the list, he was obnoxious and made a habit of "talking trash"; a regular event on most basketball teams and in most games, but not at my high school, not from a bunch of "clean-cut" White kids. Lastly and seemingly most important, he was Black. Not only was he the first Black basketball player at my high school in over a decade, he was among only 10–15 African American students in the entire school. For many of my teammates and I, he was instantly foreign in almost every way.

At first we were very proud to have someone of his talent come to our school, but as time passed and practice began, things started to unravel. I soon came to realize that he was going to take my starting position, a feeling I had yet to experience in my life. I was upset until he physically humbled me on the court just about every day in practice. So I learned to accept the fact that he was a better basketball player than I. But it didn't stop there. He was extremely cocky and his personality was very . . . Black. He sagged his shorts, pointed in your face after a good shot, and made fun of us when we weren't as graceful as he with the basketball. He listened to a different type of music, he was loud and overly confident. As days went by and the differences between us began to display themselves, we decided to put an end to it.

We ostracized him at school, but more glaring in my memory is that we systematically made sure that every time he went to the hoop he received a foul. This started out minor, but every time he bounced off the floor and talked trash, the fouls became harder. After about a week, he had had enough and he reached his breaking point. On that particular night, he must have been fouled about 20 times by various teammates. And finally, he started to cry. Here he was, the smallest, youngest, and best player on our team, completely alone, too abused to raise his usual psychological front and bearing his soul for all of us to see. He muttered a few words through his tears, he made a desperate plea for an explanation and I specifically remember him saying the following words, "Why are you doing this to me? I want to be your teammate, but I can't take this anymore."

At the time, I felt bad, as any human with feelings would, but I never really examined either of our actions. We instantly became very good friends, but that night still kind of haunts me. I remember not actually partaking in the physical abuse. I wasn't doing the fouling and I wasn't actually asking my teammates to do this, but I didn't stop it. In fact, if it had worked, I would have been the beneficiary of the starting position I had quickly lost. So I let it happen. Today in class I openly tried to find out why. I think I was so used to having the advantage in life. I didn't respect where he was coming from and I didn't know how to react to someone so different from myself. (White, male)

The family and peer groups are the most proximal collectives that influence children. These journal excerpts illustrate the pain and trauma that may accompany painting from family and peers. Names, behavior, jokes, and questions can all leave a legacy of pain, suspicion, anger, and rage. In the next chapter, we examine five other institutions that participate in the teaching of racism.

## STUDENT TESTIMONIALS

*Voices of Pain and Voices of Hope* helped me realize that I am not the only one who has to deal with racism on a daily basis. All minorities have experiences similar to the ones that I have had to deal with. In the past I would make excuses for people and their racist comments. After reading this book I knew that I could not keep my mouth closed anymore. Ignorance is no longer an excuse that I let the dominant race have.

**Kesha Alexander, Black, Female, Senior,
California State University, Northridge**

*Voices of Pain and Voices of Hope* opened my eyes to insidious racism that permeates our society. The book brought me to a new understanding about the ways young people who are not White can be harmed. As a lifelong resident of the diverse city of Los Angeles, I considered myself aware of racial discrimination yet as a White person I was in fact only aware of the more obvious. For me, the personal stories in Dr. Rabow's book make his points especially poignant. The understanding I gained from this book has translated into more conscious words, thoughts, and actions. As someone who volunteers in public schools and interacts with diverse populations of young people, I am immensely grateful.

**Jill Ash, White, Female, University of California,
Los Angeles Graduate**

*Voices of Pain and Voices of Hope* was the catalyst to the healing process in my life. When I began to read about the experiences that other students of color, men, and women had, it validated and confirmed the feelings that I had all my life. These were feelings of frustration and fear. As I began reading these accounts, I began feeling a bond with others that I had never felt before. The feelings that arose from reading the stories of others helped me acknowledge the common bonds that I now feel towards all. By capturing the voices of pain, Jerome Rabow helps us find the voices of hope.

**Erron Brumfield, African American Male, UCLA Graduate**

As an earnest student of ethnic studies and race relations, and as a woman of color who was raised to embrace diversity, I had previously considered myself to be a "non-painter"—clean, absolved, and innocent of any form of prejudice. While I thought *Voices of Pain, Voices of Hope* would be an interesting read of my schoolmates' anecdotes and perspectives, I did not think I would personally gain anything from it.

However, *Voices* reminded me that dominant and subordinate relationships are not restricted to White, heterosexual males versus the rest of us. I soon realized, for example, I'd already begun to develop an elitist attitude towards those less educated than myself; I, too, had unconsciously wielded a paintbrush. Hence, this book, while absolutely crucial for White students, is nevertheless valuable to those of us who think we already "get" it.

**Malina K. Koani-Guzman, Native Hawaiian, Female, Graduate,
University of California, Los Angeles, Law Student**

Dr. Jerome Rabow's book, *Voices of Pain and Voices of Hope,* is a text that explores the diversity of individuals across the globe. When I first skimmed the pages of this book I figured that it was just another professor-written, professor-assigned text. When I really took the time to read the book in its entirety I began to feel sympathetic to the experiences of those individuals who filled the pages with their stories. Each story left a mark, each story left me seeking meaning and answers, each account of discrimination left me inspired to change the nature of human relations. The text is composed of commentary presented by Dr. Rabow and the personal accounts of individuals who have been exposed to the unjust and discriminatory practices of an ignorant world. Rabow's text becomes effective for the reader because the material is derived from years of research that includes all diverse groups; it is an all-inclusive text. When you read through the personal accounts that fill the pages you begin to feel connected with each story; the individual accounts leave an impression that will be difficult to forget. Rabow's approach to creating this text is ahead of its time in that he is more concerned with sharing other people's stories and exposing the flaws of narrow-minded thinking, rather that concerning himself with personal discourse on the subject matter.

**Shane Underwood, California State University, Northridge, 2004**

# II

## *Learning to Paint:*
### *Institutional Settings*

Though a great deal of painting is learned from families and peers, there are many "others" in society whom we have encountered that are instrumental in teaching us how to become painters. These "others" reside in all institutions, looking for impressionable subjects to teach their racist strokes. In the journals we found five institutional settings that were repeatedly mentioned by the students as providing instruction on how to paint. The norms that govern these institutions, norms that ensure power and privilege of Whites and racism for people of color, will not be documented in this book. Rather, we will offer the reader examples that occur within our everyday institutions. Specifically, students referred to schools, media, law enforcement, workplaces, and public settings as being key areas for preserving and perpetuating racism.

## I. SCHOOL

The school environment serves many functions for children as they develop. It is in the school that children learn educational skills, independence, socialization with peers, and numerous other skills that will follow them through life. However, it is also in the school that children learn about racism. After all, the school arena is made up of human beings, teachers, counselors, psychologists, social workers, and administrators who often have not confronted their own stereotypes and prejudice. Additionally, the school is made up of children who are already learning about racism from family members, peers, and others. According to "The Review of Higher Education," it is estimated that a total of one million bias incidents occur every year on U.S. campuses (Tolerance.org, 2001). The school environment is an active breeding ground for teaching children to become painters as well as the subjects to be painted.

Teachers have the ability and resources to shape the minds of their students. Though it is our hope that most educators use their tremendous power and influence in the classroom to dispel myths, stereotypes, and prejudices involving race, this is not always the case. Instead, teachers are often the painters of racism; they can hold impressionable minds hostage to their damaging ideologies. When teachers instill racism in students, this teaches White students that it is acceptable to paint, while teaching minority students that they should be painted. In the following examples, a White teacher and a White counselor impose their low expectations upon two students of color. In the first example, a high school counselor treats a Latina, who is eager to turn over a new leaf and to start college life, as a person who could not possibly succeed. The counselor not only misperceives her ethnicity but also can't believe that this student does not wish to get married right after high school and have babies.

I finally built enough courage to speak to my high school counselor about college. That week, I had overheard a couple of seniors discussing community college. They assured me that high school transcripts are not given to the college; it would be a new beginning. Thus, I made an appointment with my counselor to share this revelation that I was experiencing of dedicating myself to attending community college. I anticipated that he would be excited and encourage me to pursue my academic dreams.

When I arrived at his office, he was buried in a newspaper and refused to look up. He assumed that a teacher had sent me to his office for disrupting the class. After I assured him this was not the case, he proceeded to remind me that I should be in class and not wasting time. "I want to go to college," I blurted out.

He finally put down his newspaper and stared at me for a few minutes. I held my breath and awaited his response. Strangely, a smile began to form. Finally, I thought, I have made him happy and excited about my future. But then he covered his mouth after letting out a slight chuckle. "You know Ms. M," he said. "You are not qualified to go to a 4-year university straight out of high school. This school provides information to serious students about college and I think you know you are not one of them." He reached into his desk, pulled out my transcript, and plopped it in front of me.

"Now, let me ask you, do you know of any university that accepts students who have wasted 4 years accumulating C's and D's?" He proceeded, "Let me remind you that you need to focus on graduating. And besides, aren't you Mexican?"

"No!" I snapped. "I'm from Chile."

"Oh," he replied. "Isn't that the same thing? I mean, isn't it part of the Hispanic culture for females to get married and have children as soon as you turn 18?"

For a moment, I couldn't quite understand what he was (and was not) saying. I knew some Mexican young women who had children, but I also knew White, African American, and Asian young women who had had children as well. I looked deeper into his cold face. My face began to get hot and tears formed in my eyes. I bravely swallowed my tears and said, "Look, I didn't come here to discuss my culture with you. I would like to receive more information on community college."

He took a deep breath and sat quietly for a moment. Finally he said, "Ms. M, I'm glad that you are thinking about your future. I'm going to be brutally honest with you because it is obvious that no one else is providing you with direction. You will remain trapped in the unmotivated life that you lead and the people you surround yourself with forever. I am certain that you are going to get yourself pregnant within years after you graduate."

"How could you say that to me? You don't even know who I am!"

I stormed out of his office and ran to the furthest part of campus. I cried out all the confusion and hurt and recognized that I had been looking at myself through the eyes of those who despised my skin. And so I began the lifelong journey of finding comfort with people with my own skin. (Latina, female)

In the next excerpt a Latina student comments about the stereotyping by a White teacher towards an Asian student. The teacher cannot believe that the student has tried very hard to complete the work successfully. She discredits the student's efforts because of the belief she has of Asians as the "model minority." The student acknowledges that she held the same stereotypes as the teacher.

In fourth or fifth grade, I can remember a teacher responding to an Asian boy based on his race. It was not just a one-time thing but a constant stream of comments about his mathematical ability. I guess he had problems with the math content, which went against the stereotype she had of Asian students. One time when passing back the test she told him that "he must not have tried his best because you guys always get A's." The poor kid mumbled something quietly about studying really hard for the test, but the teacher did not hear him. Another time the teacher commented to the same boy that "Sara got a better grade than you and she is not even Oriental." I did not say anything when this happened because at that point of my life I totally had the same stereotype of Asians and their math ability. (Latina, female)

In the next excerpt, an African American woman discusses her experiences with racism in both public and private school settings.

At my ethnically diverse public high school, our principal—an old White man—made a rule that students couldn't walk together in groups larger than three because more than three of us together was intimidating. He reasoned that if large groups of us (I think I remember the words "hoodlums" or "thugs" being used) invoked fear in him, then certainly some of the smaller or more timid students would be scared of us, and the school should be an environment where everyone felt safe.

While it was never overtly said, large segments of the student body were people of color. When students were released from class, large groups of visibly Filipino, Samoan, Black, Latino, Asian, and White students would congregate in their chosen home bases on campus. The White students on campus seldom had to feel the burn of the pepper spray the authorities commonly sprayed to break up a fight. Nicer areas of the city didn't have anything like our version of discipline. Once this new rule was implemented, though it seemed ludicrous to me—a well-behaved 14-year-old—I quickly found out that the new rule wasn't a joke.

Sitting with my predominantly Black crowd of friends in our usual hangout having lunch, we quickly made a group larger than three. The police didn't bother us at first, as many students crowded together in their usual hangouts; there were only so many places to eat. Whenever we stood up to walk somewhere in a group of more than three, an officer would quickly approach us with their pepper spray drawn, and would tell us to spread immediately. After an officer threatened my friends and I with pepper spray (a group of four petite Black girls) as if we were criminals, I decided to avoid walking anywhere anymore.

But the threats were inescapable. The next day, the moment the bell signaled the end of lunch, the police again came to where we were sitting comfortably and threatened us with their pepper spray drawn and ready to shoot. "Disperse," they said. We quickly grabbed our backpacks and ran to class. At the same time, I saw a group of Latino students being assaulted in the same fashion.

I went to a predominantly White private school until the sixth grade. "Predominantly White" meaning that I was usually the only minority child in my grade, and I don't remember there being more than five Black students at the school during any time when I was there. So I faced social isolation as a Black child. I was always different, could not possibly fit in, and had grown up feeling so much like an outcast and against the norm. So when I suddenly moved to a public multiethnic middle school, I still didn't fit in. Not only was I different because I was a "goody goody" private school kid, but I was a Black girl socialized to be White. Since I had gone to school with nothing but White kids my whole life, I didn't know what it was to be acculturated as a "Black girl."

Upon arriving at the public school, my peers wondered at me, painting me with their expectations of what a Black girl should be. "Why do you talk so proper?" they asked repeatedly. "Why do you act White?" I did well in school easily, but my self-esteem dropped. "You're not like other black girls, you're the nicest Black kid I've ever met." "You are so gifted and bright," the teachers told me again and again, as if they couldn't believe it. (African American, female)

Another student recalls how her elementary school teacher taught her that as an Asian, she could not be an American. For this painter, being American was equated with being White.

I remember asking my teacher when I was in elementary school, if I was White. I wanted to draw myself using the white crayon. But my teacher said that White people were Americans. So my question was: "What's an American?" To that my teacher replied, "they have white skin, they speak English, and they were born here." To a little kid, the underside of my arms and my stomach certainly look white to me. Plus, I was born here, and I also spoke English. But I couldn't understand why I wasn't considered White. My teacher told me I was Yellow and I should use the yellow crayon. I drew myself with the yellow crayon, but my skin didn't match the yellow crayon. To this day, I don't think I've ever found a shade that matches my skin color. (Asian, female)

Another Asian female recalls how she internalized the message that she was stupid in kindergarten because she spoke little English. Moreover, her teacher instilled in her the image of White beauty.

When I entered kindergarten, I spoke virtually no English (although I understood it to a large degree). But because I spoke no English, other kids and some teachers treated me like I was stupid. As a child, I wanted so badly NOT to be Asian. I wanted to look like the people on television and speak perfect English. The only role model I saw for myself on television was Wonder Woman, who with her dark hair, I imagined, was part Asian. A strong, but similar kind of prejudice against myself came in the form of a doll. I wanted so bad to have blond hair and blue eyes like Barbie. And it was always painfully obvious to me that I couldn't be without major expense. My friends from school in Irvine were all White with light-colored hair and blue or green eyes. I remember when the teacher would make comments about how some girls had pretty eyes and golden curls were always the prettiest. My mother always reminded me that I would "always have yellow skin." But I couldn't do anything about it, unless I took it to the point of totally reconstructing my face and body. Regardless, as a child, you don't have much choice (though nowadays, with plastic surgery, almost anything is possible). When I was 10, I talked about getting blue contacts, dying my hair, and getting breast implants and artificial legs because I hated my Asian features. I don't know when I grew out of this, but this was a childhood fantasy of mine. I hated myself so much that when one of my aunts bought me an Asian doll that looked like me for my birthday, I threw it away the next day. (Chinese, female)

Teachers are not the only painters on school grounds. As stated previously, the peer group is extremely potent in influencing its members, particularly when young. Painful and damaging messages are often transmitted to those that appear different from the clique. Also, as children have not learned the more manipulative and subtle skills involved in political correctness, their racism is usually uncensored, raw, and extremely cruel.

In the following excerpt, a Latina student recalls her fourth-grade experience with racism inflicted by her peers in the classroom. Specifically, because of her brown skin, her peers gave her a bar of soap to wash off her less-than-White skin color.

> In elementary school, I was an ugly little thing, or at least, I thought I was. I was tall for my age, too skinny, and I had big, puffy hair. It wasn't that I was teased about it, it was more that the boys did not like me. It made it even worse that my sister and cousin were in the same school, and they were considered to be the prettiest girls around. The worst part about me, I thought, was my skin color. This is exactly how my classmates felt about me. One day, in the fourth grade, someone placed a little box in front of my desk. I looked into it and saw a bar of soap and a bottle of water. There was a note that said something like, "go wash yourself and scrub that dirt off." I felt really bad and wished that I could be as light as my cousin C. She always got all the attention because she had blonde hair and light eyes. Being dark in my school, or even in my neighborhood, taught me that I was ugly and that no one would ever like me. (Latina, female)

In the following excerpt, an African American male discusses how prejudice occurred in the confines of his school. Specifically, he recalls that when he was in third grade a peer taught him about racism when he called him a derogatory name.

> I first learned of racism outside my home. I learned it because I had to deal with it as an everyday struggle. It became particularly prevalent when I was in the third grade, and my friend called me a "nigger." Being called a "nigger" was the equivalent of stabbing me in the heart. Here I am, playing with this kid, whom I consider a friend and equal, and he has the audacity to call me a "nigger!" I did not know exactly what the word meant but I knew it was degrading. No one should ever dare to call a Black person a "nigger." Those days of oppression should be over. I was only 9 years old, but my blood was boiling and its temperature was rising because this kid was prejudiced. (African American, male)

The media augments the racist messages that students learn in schools from teachers and peers.

## II. THE MEDIA

The entertainment industry surrounds us with images of fair-skinned, blond-haired, and blue-eyed picture-perfect actors, models and singers. The media's treatment of children of color has a two-fold function. Its depiction of one-dimensional beauty teaches its own about privilege while simultaneously teaching those who are different that they are inferior in their uniqueness. Moreover, even if the media chooses to present difference, it does so cleverly by still maintaining its one-dimensional image of beauty. Specifically, if minorities are used they will still model the uniform ideal of Whiteness. In other words, if African Americans or Latinos are represented, they will only be chosen if their skin color is atypically light. Indeed, in the May 2001 edition of *People's 50 Most Beautiful People,* the chosen few were almost exclusively White. While one may dismiss the importance of this particular magazine, its message is extremely potent; namely, the most beautiful people in the world are White. We could even go a step further and argue that the true symbolic message here is that only White people are beautiful. Moreover, *People Magazine* is not alone in its depiction of White beauty. On the contrary, this overrepresentation of Whites can be found in all of our magazines of choice from *Vogue* to *Vanity Fair* to *The New Yorker.*

Additionally, the entertainment industry, with its one-dimensional image of beauty, enjoys a pervasive nature that reaches us all, particularly those of us who do not fit its image of perfection. While White children flip through the pages of *People Magazine,* their own positive self-image is affirmed and simultaneously confirms their place of privilege. They are "in" the pictures and scenes of wealth, happiness, and comfort. However, people of color are rarely included. When they are depicted they tend to have White features. Although most women suffer or feel envious when viewing these pictures, envy about weight is fixable. Envy of someone's skin color or eye shape is not modifiable. This experience is completely different for the non-White child, who yearns to identify with the images presented in this magazine. This latter child desperately searches for the one person who looks like them in terms of physical features. When the child realizes that there is no one chosen as "beautiful" resembling them or their race, then great pain, isolation, and feelings of inferiority and powerlessness are invoked. In the following excerpt, a Filipina discusses how Asian faces were simply not present on television when she was growing up. Therefore, she was forced to shape her own identity based on the White characteristics that she was bombarded with by the media.

> All the faces I saw on television were White and Black. Asian faces were invisible. I modeled my identity from the characteristics that I was constantly being exposed to. (Filipina, female)[1]

---

[1]There are differing opinions concerning the use of the terms "Filipino" or "Philipino." Some Philipino Americans believe that the term Filipino symbolizes the subjugation of the Philippines by colonial powers since the *f* sound is not used in native Filipino dialects. Others reject the change of term because it may be confusing and imply that they cannot pronounce the *f* sound. Because a student's identity awareness was often not indicated, the term "Filipino" shall be used throughout the book.

The media's emphasis on Whiteness can be very damaging as it brainwashes minority children into viewing themselves as inferior or less desirable. In the following excerpt, an African American woman describes how the media has impacted her. The student is so unaccustomed to seeing Black actors engaged in love scenes that when presented with this rarity she actually finds it "gross."

> I remember thinking that love scenes between two Black actors were gross, I didn't want to watch it but I could watch two White actors without a problem." (African American, female)

In the next excerpt, a Chicano male describes how he internalized the media images of Whiteness as the superior ideal.

> I mean how can you not want to be like the guys on TV commercials, or on billboards, these are guys I would refer to as "firme" in Spanish. What else could a young man want to be like if that is all he sees being advertised as attractive. Even today, as I walk along campus and see White guys and how some resemble the images on TV, I continue to believe that they look better. (Chicano, male)

Moreover, an Arab male recalls how the media's depiction of sameness affected his self-image and created a desire to deny his cultural roots and very identity.

> My attitude was that if only I looked more like them, then I could rule the world . . . I unfortunately have to admit that I desperately wanted to deny my own cultural roots and identity and immerse myself in and become the White culture I saw on TV and at school. (Arab, male)

In the following excerpt, an African American female recalls how the media only depicted light-skinned Blacks as worthy of attaining fame and fortune.

> Growing up I was secretly told that the darker the skin tones, the deeper the problems. Not by my parents, but by my peer group and my surroundings, the billboards, the commercials, ads, beauty queens. If he/she was Black, famous, and had money they were "light skinned." (African American, female)

As we have indicated earlier, institutions reinforce each other in their message of racism. In the following example, a young woman describes how school, peers, and the media taught her about herself.

> I knew since elementary school that it was not desirable to be Chinese. It was there that Chinese people were unpopular and looked down upon. I knew that by the way people would talk about us or imitate us. Aside from the typical slant-eyed faces that I watched non-Asian kids make, I always heard kids making fun of the Chinese language by caricaturizing it in their

imitation. And this continued on into intermediate school (grades 5–8). This, of course, did not stop when I left school. At home I would see the same caricatures on TV. (Chinese, female)

A classic Disney movie is also a cause of self-hatred for a young Asian woman.

When I first saw the animated movie, "Little Mermaid," I instantly fell in love with the movie and the songs. I fell in love with Ariel, the mermaid and her prince charming. I would watch the movie over and over again. As I watched these animated movies when I was 13 years old, I had a hard time accepting who I was and what I looked like. I thought to myself, "Why do I look like this? Why can't I look like Ariel?" Even my friends were always ranting and raving about her pretty hair, voice, and figure. We knew it was just a cartoon. However, the thought did not occur to me that Ariel was a drawing, and most White girls do not even look nearly as pretty. However, to me, having a nice figure, long wavy hair that blew in the wind, big eyes, and a voice of an angel would make me the most beautiful person in the world.

I decided that I was going to look like Ariel even if it killed me. I wanted a beautiful figure and a beautiful face. I was determined that during the summer vacation, I would look like Ariel and then when I made the transition to high school, my friends would be shocked and I would just impress the world. It was then that I decided that I would stop eating to make my figure look like the animated drawings that depicted the ideal beauty in my eyes. I lost over 20 pounds in the 2 months of vacation. I put nothing in my stomach, except water. I was ready to die because I wanted to look beautiful, and in order for me to look beautiful I thought I had to look like those White models on television, the movies, magazines, or even animated movies. I had to have a figure like them. I had to be tall and skinny. Because of my irrational thought and my irrational decision, I lost a huge part of my life. (Asian, female)

In the next excerpt a Chinese male describes what he believes to be the media messages for Asian men and Asian women. He understands the historical treatment of Black women by the media and suggests that Asian women are the new forbidden beauties.

My Asian brothers are taught by the media to hate ourselves. We are taught to look in the mirror and despise our slanted eyes, our yellow skin, and our pudgy nose. We are told that we have small penises. We are told that we perform so badly in bed that the Asian women need to turn to the White man for sexual satisfaction. We are taught to think that we are ugly. And guess what? It worked. Most Asian men internalized it. It saddens me when the males of a race think that they are so ugly, and believe me, this sentiment comes out whether it is subtle or someone is simply joking—it comes out, and it saddens me. We are also taught that we will never be quite as good as White men. We are taught that White women are the epitome of beauty, and that we will never be able to have them. My Asian sisters, you are taught to be sexy for the White man. You are exotic; you are submissive; you are great in bed. You are taught to fawn over White men, because they are perfect in ways that Asian men are not. You are taught to despise your culture; dye your hair blond; wear blue contacts; and stand next to the White man, so that you might be a little lighter, a little more accepted, A LITTLE MORE WHITE. Your delicate, exotic beauty is your special sexual pass into mainstream acceptance, but only when you accept the stream of the White man's semen. This society has raped your body and mind, and left it covered in the sticky ejaculation of submission, of fawning, of bleach. I can go into a million theories why this phenomenon occurs in American society, but in the end, most agree that it is just another expression of White male privilege. In this, and many other historical cases, it translates into sexual politics. These stereotypes have been branded on us. And while Asian women get the better deal, it is still a stereotype that has been given, and not created, and can be taken back whenever society pleases. Any stereotype is a bad stereotype. Once, Black women were forbidden and White men pursued them. In our generation, it is the Asian woman's turn to be raped (Chinese, male)

A student begins to recognize how being White has afforded him with privileges not similarly shared by other races, particularly regarding representation in the media. This male begins to question the overrepresentation of Whites on television, in movies, in newspapers and in magazines. More importantly, he questions what the lack of minority representation in the media must feel like for other races.

I was completely unaware of my privilege as a dominant group member of an oppressive society. I thought that my life experiences were the same as all the others, never thinking about race. When I walked into a store and received plenty of help and paid with a credit card and wasn't even asked for identification, I thought that is how it is for everyone. I never realized that if my Black friend walked into the store, she may have been watched suspiciously and asked for several forms of identification before her check was accepted. It never even entered my mind that band-aids are supposed to be skin colored, but they really only matched my white flesh. I never realized that what I saw in the media were people of my race, and what it would feel like to be a minority who only sees Whites on TV, in the movies, in the newspaper, and in magazines. When I was searching for an apartment last year, I never had to think about the fact that someone would not want to rent to me because of my race. (White, male)

In the next example, a White female describes her previous assessment of Black magazines as an example of self-segregation.

I never understood why magazines like *Ebony* were popular. I thought that Black people were further alienating themselves, by creating a separate magazine, instead of subscribing to the "general" magazine. I did not realize that these "general" magazines are simply White magazines. Now I see a woman's magazine and not only see the size of the models, but the color. In flipping through, I see mostly Caucasian models, with an occasional "token" light-skinned minority. The make up advice is obviously geared towards White women, and most of the hairstyle suggestions would never work on someone who does not have Caucasian hair. Occasionally a magazine will show one hairstyle for African-American women, but this is a side-note, instead of the rule. (White, female)

## III. LAW ENFORCEMENT

Law enforcement officials are typically extremely humane and courageous persons who risk their lives every day to ensure safety for all. However, as is true of every profession, there are some officials who maintain racist ideals and prejudices against certain minority groups. The only difference between a racist policeman and any other racist professional is that the former typically has greater power to abuse under the guise of the law than the latter. Sometimes this power turns deadly.

Most Whites learn of police racism and brutality through the public exposure generated by the Rodney Kings of the world. Whites have little firsthand experience with being harassed, beaten, and even murdered at the hands of the police. This is part of that privilege enjoyed by Whites. However, this is not the experience of other races, particularly African Americans and Latinos who often report feeling targeted by law enforcement because of their skin color. In the following excerpt, an African American student describes the fear that the police instilled in him when he was handcuffed on the ground and told that he might be a possible shooting suspect simply because of his race.

I still have fear going through the wrong neighborhoods at times, not so much because of the people, but because of the police. In a sense, I never feel safe when I drive. I have always had a fear of the police because of the power they possess. I have had only one run-in with the police and it was major. I was riding with a friend who lived near me and all of a sudden the police were right behind us. We had three people in the back seat, and one of them lived in the predominantly White neighborhood near our school. As we turned off of the main street onto the residential neighborhood, they turned on their sirens and pulled us over. While I was wondering what we could have possibly done wrong, two officers behind their car with their guns drawn asked us to put our hands up. I was handcuffed on the ground and explained that we were possible suspects of a shooting, which occurred earlier that day. It was one of the most humiliating and scary experiences that I've ever had in my life. They checked our car for weapons and only found schoolbooks. They had to let us go. There looked to be a White woman in the first police car trying to identify us. This did not make me feel very good because I heard one of the cops say that they were looking for a black, gray, or blue car with 2–5 Black male passengers. And they really thought that they would find the people who did this. How many people fit that description? I felt like I was a threat to society. (African American, male)

Another student recalls his frightening run-in with the police. Specifically, this African American male and his friend were stopped, told to get out of their car, and then instructed to get on the ground with their legs spread. The reason for the interrogation was the same as in the previous example: skin color.

Out of nowhere a cop car came behind us and began flashing its lights. We were pretty shocked because it was so sudden. We were told to get out of the car with our hands up. We were then told to get on the ground with our legs spread. At this point I had no idea what was going on and my feelings of being intimidated slowly turned to feelings of anger and resentment. They had absolutely no right to conduct this procedure on us. They checked to see if we had illegal substances on us. They looked at my ID and checked my background and they found that I was clean. Knowing this, they let me go on the curb. My best friend however, did not receive the same fate. He did not have his ID on him so they began questioning him about a million things such as where he was from, what was his address, where he went to school, if he was in a gang, and whether he had any tattoos, just to name a few. After about a half hour of trying to figure out who he was, the police officers decided to let us go. Before leaving the scene I demanded a reason as to why we were put under such circumstances. He said that the car we were sitting in (which belonged to me) "fit the description of a vehicle stolen earlier in the day" and that my friend "fit the description" of a youth they had been after for burglary and drug dealing for quite some time. (African American, male)

In this next excerpt, a White student recalls how he and his Black friends were both painted. A policeman tries to teach the White student that he should not be socializing with African Americans. What is surprising about this example of racism is that the officer was himself an African American.

I remember a time I went with some of my Black friends to a high school football game. At the game there were some police officers that made sure nothing happened after the game. My friends and me were standing around after the game just talking. I remember seeing a Black officer staring at us. I thought he was going to question us because one of my friends was drunk, talking loud, and being obnoxious. The Black cop mentioned for me to go over to him. I went to him, and he looked at my friends and then me and asked me what I was doing with them. I was so shocked by this question that I asked him to repeat it. I was not sure what he meant by it. "They're Black and you're White, what are you doing with them?" I searched his face for some sort of hint that he was joking or being sarcastic, but he was serious. Shocked, I simply said, "They're my friends!" And proceeded to go back to them. I felt so many emotions that night. A Black officer asked me why I was hanging out with a bunch of Black guys. To me, it made no difference what color they were, but for some reason, the fact that they were Black and I was White was important to him. I could not understand why he would question my association with them. For the first time in my life, I knew what it felt like to have my actions questioned simply because of my skin color and who I was with. (Bicultural, White/Armenian American, male)

In the following excerpt, a Chicano student describes his experience with suspicion and mistrust by the police. A medical emergency is neglected and the stereotype of Latinos and Indians as drug users is implemented.

After chatting for a while, my friends and I decided to go out to a bar near the beach. We were all happy, none of us had been drinking, and all we wanted was to enjoy the time we had available because it is rare when we have the opportunity to spend time together. So we drove off expecting to have a good time. Suddenly, the driver began to have convulsions and the car went out of control. After we got control of the car we immediately dialed 911 and we all exited the car. I followed directions from the dispatcher. He was unconscious, shaking, and foam was coming out of his mouth. The paramedics came to the rescue and took control of the situation. They asked questions and we cooperated with them. Minutes later, the police arrived. They saw a new car with three Latinos and a Hindu lying on the ground out of control. They assumed it was a drug overdose and began searching the car and interrogating us. One police officer pulled me aside and began asking questions.

"Have you been doing drugs?" he asked. I answered, "I just got back from UCLA, I'm a student there, I don't do drugs and we haven't been drinking." While this was taking place, the second officer kept searching the car, in hope of finding some illegal substance. At the end of the night, we all came to the conclusion that the police officers were not concerned with the well-being of our friend. When they first arrived they saw three Mexicans panicking and in shock. They assumed this was a drug-related incident and wanted to find evidence. Despite my effort to cooperate with him I was confronted with prejudice. I found that these officers who are supposed to serve and protect did no such thing. Instead, what I encountered was racial profiling and intimidation. (Chicano, male)

This last example of a police encounter with a student reads like a horror movie. It starts out with friends hoping to celebrate Christmas Eve until the police arrive and threaten the lives of the Black young men who are waiting outside. Fortunately, this story does not end with gun shots, but rather with a sarcastic farewell.

When I was 19 years old, some friends and I went to a mutual friend's house to celebrate the Christmas Eve holiday. When we got there, he wasn't home yet so we stood near my friend's car while waiting for him to arrive. While we were waiting, a police car drove by and shined their lights on us. I immediately had that "here we go again" feeling come over me. It was commonplace in 1995 for police to interrogate people on sight in Baldwin Hills. So when the police shined their lights on us, no one was surprised. During that period in my life, I was probably pulled over and searched about once every 2 weeks. As a result, I resented the police with a passion. They made me feel like I was some kind of threat to society.

Two Black police officers exited the car with their guns drawn and ordered us to put our hands in the air. We did. The officers then approached us and frisked us individually. Once they found out that we had no weapons, they asked us to put our hands on the hood of the car. They then emptied our pockets and went through our wallets to take our driver's licenses to run our names through the computer to see if we had any warrants. The younger officer kept referring to the older officer as "pop," and the older officer called the younger one "son." When I noticed that they had different last names, I realized that they were going through some kind of sick bad-cop/good-cop routine. While we were waiting for our names to clear, they started to tell us how much they hated car thieves.

"Pop, there's nothing like whooping a car thief's ass," said the younger one.

When we tried to explain that we were in front of a friend's house, we were told to "shut the fuck up." It turned out that a warrant for both myself and a friend came back on the computer. We had both forgotten to pay a traffic ticket.

"Ah, they steal cars and don't pay tickets," said the older one.

They began to tell us how much they hate gangsters, and claimed that they beat up two of them about an hour ago. They said all the local "bloods" know not to "fuck" with them. I had heard many threats made by police before, but something about the tone of their voices scared me. It was like you could tell that they were telling the truth. Perhaps it's just a stereotype of mine, but it seems like some Black cops feel like they can get away with more brutality against other Blacks simply because they are the same color. The younger officer then looked at me while putting a hand on his gun and said, "Go ahead, run away." I didn't know if he was testing me or letting me go. The blank stares on their faces told me that they were just as unsure as I was. Knowing that my friends were scared too only made me more frightened.

"It's a good thing you didn't run, cuz I would've blown the back of your head off," said the younger officer, with a grin on his face. (African American, male)

# IV. THE WORKPLACE

In addition to the influence of the media, school environment, and law enforcement officials, students also recalled learning to be painters when they entered the workforce. In the following example a White female remembers her duties working at a club in West Hollywood. A major part of her job was to promote racism per strict orders from her boss.

> I worked at a very high-end club in West Hollywood, called the G. I was the VIP host for an exclusive room, so it was my job to decide who could and could not come in. My manager would often, very often, come and yell at me because I had let too many Persians in the room and/or that the room looked like shit because I had let unattractive women and men up there. I used to really cringe when he said these things, but I heard it all the time and I was expected to enforce his racist and "lookism" standards. And he had the same rationale, that the rich White people would not want to come up there and spend a lot of money if there were not good looking women and people of the "right" race up there. I only stayed because I made a tremendous amount of money, bigwigs tipping me for reservations and/or tables, in this very sought-after club. But I didn't have my soul while I was there. Every night I would come home upset about things that occurred. I just can't believe that Persians and Arabs are so discriminated against in Los Angeles, and even worse that I was a part of it. I perpetuated being the oppressor in this way and perpetuated racism by thinking twice before I let "too" many Arabs into the VIP room. Oh, I just remembered, he was even worse about Blacks. They usually never even made it in the club at all, and into where I was. There were a limited number of Black regulars, but of course they were either well connected or had money. I was yelled at for letting too many Blacks into the room as well. Basically, I was in the position that would discriminate against all unattractive people unless they were "somebody" or had lots of money, and all races, except Whites. I eventually quit and I've never walked into a club since. (White, female)

Similarly, another student describes how African American customers were treated in the store in which he worked. Specifically, this student, also an African American, recalls how people of color were suspected of stealing and thus watched and scrutinized at every turn to the point of actually demanding to look at the contents in their bags. What is most concerning about this example is that this racist ideology regarding the trustworthiness of African Americans briefly caused this student to view members of his own race as thieves solely based on their skin color.

> I was seeing discrimination take place at my work almost twice a week. People of color are seen as not being able to pay for many of the articles that they try on. Since the area that I work in is very wealthy there are not that many people of color that come into the store. It seems that when they

do my manager tells everyone to keep an eye on them. I've often heard the other employees say that the reason why they watch them is because they look suspicious. After a period of time I too began to feel and think that the people of color that came into my store were stealing. But I never thought that I'd see what I saw during the holidays. I was working in the afternoon with the manager and one of the employees when a group of three black males entered the store. Two of which were carrying big bags. The manager quickly came over to us and told us to keep an eye out. After they perused the store for about 20 minutes and were about to leave, the manager went over to them and asked to look into their bags. They did not seem as though this was the first time it had happened to them because they simply opened it up and let her examine the contents. She did not find anything from our store so she politely said sorry and they left. (African American, male)

In the next example, an Asian female discusses how she learned the culture of racism when she worked as a waitress. Her coworkers taught her to predict her tip based on the customer's race.

All of us who wait on tables think that we can look at the customers and predict the kind of tip we will receive and this makes it hard to approach each table with the same enthusiasm. The general consensus at my work is that African Americans are the worst tippers. There are always exceptions and then I feel bad for having thought differently. But the majority of African American customers are very hard to wait on. They seem very demanding, they complain about their food and send it back, their alcoholic beverages are too watered down and regardless of the amount of their bill—10 dollars or 40 dollars, the tip is always the same—1 dollar. A guy at my work who is Black himself started the phrase "groove dollar." He even says that most Black people do not tip well. (Asian, female)

In this last excerpt, a Latina student pays the price for being assertive. Specifically, as an unsatisfied customer in a florist shop, this student asks to speak with the manager and is faced with raw racism.

"May I help you?" "As a matter of fact, yes you can. You see my cousin here had ordered a simple bouquet. I just want a bouquet that's ready but just add a rose. Just one simple rose." She smiled and sighed, "You see hon, I don't think that's possible." I smiled and replied, "Isn't that what florists do though? Can I ask your manager to see what he or she thinks a florist does?" At that point I felt a tug at my dress and my cousin whispered that it was all right, and to drop the request. As I turned once again towards the florist, she was beginning to dismantle a bouquet and she inserted a rose in the middle. As she did she murmured something I would never forget. "You can't just come in and ask for something, damn Mexicans!" That really insulted me, and I didn't want to argue with her anymore. I told her to excuse me as I proceeded to look for the manager. As I found him I told him that I wanted service and how I felt personally insulted as a person of color by the florist. As we both walked towards the florist the bouquet was done. She told me the amount and asked "Cash?" "Credit please." I smiled. But I knew that it was too good to be true, to just pay and leave. And as we left, I heard some remarks that just showed me that racism is alive everywhere. "Go back to where you came from. Lazy mother-fuckers, just come here to cause trouble." I turned around as the store stayed behind, and I saw a little boy look me in the eyes saying "SPICK!" (Mexican American, female)

In this woman's excerpt there are three painters. There is the employee who has painted the student a "lazy mother-fucker" simply because of her race. There is a manager whose silence allows the painting to occur. More frightening, however, is the child bystander who has already learned to paint blatant strokes of racism.

## V. PUBLIC SETTINGS

Occasionally, the learning and teaching of racism occurs in public settings. Feagin has described how people of color receive racist comments in restaurants, retail outlets, on public transportation, as well as in open public places (Feagin, 1991). Strangers often feel that they have the right and need to instruct others.

A donut shop is the scene of a public lesson in racism. A customer levies his racism at a Cambodian student working in her parents' store.

When I tell people that I am Cambodian, they automatically assume that we are dirty people, killers, and deviants because of our past history with the Pol Pot and Khmer Rouge. People judge me on the basis of my ethnicity even before they get to know who I am, which makes me annoyed at them for prejudging me. Two to three weeks ago, when I was working at my parent's Donut Shop, a customer of ours, an elderly Persian man in his sixties, asked me about the kind of food I eat. I told him the usual kinds of food: beef, pork, chicken, vegetables, and fruits. The same type of food everyone eats, it is just cooked and prepared differently from American food. Then, out of nowhere he asked me, "Do you eat dog?" I was shocked and mortified at even the thought of eating a dog. I could not believe that he just asked me that ridiculous question. The question was a surprise attack on me. How can someone accuse another person of such a horrible act of animal cruelty? To say the least, I was dumbfounded. "Was he joking or was he serious about it?" I mumbled to myself. I asked him if he was joking and he said, "No." I told him, "I never ate a dog in my whole life and I would never eat one in the future either." I asked him why he asked me that and he said, "I thought all Asians ate dogs." I told him, "People would only eat cats and dogs if they were desperate for food and they had nothing else to eat." This was what I had to say in defense of all Asians. That was enough for me; my opinion about him dropped tenfold. He incorrectly judged and insulted me, and on top of that, all other Cambodian and Asian people on the planet too. I was at a loss for words. Afterwards, I realized that he did not know any better; that is why he said those words, out of ignorance and myths. Probably, nobody has ever taken the time to tell him that dogs are not a popular entree in Asia. I hope he has corrected his misguided idea after our conversation. I am still shaken by his words. Now, I walk around thinking if other people think I eat dogs. (Cambodian, female)

For most of us, family members, peer groups, the media, teachers, law enforcement officials, and persons in the workforce have exposed us to explicit and implicit racism. These painters teach us that difference is usually "lesser." None of us can escape or even ignore the previous teachings of the painters in our lives. Moreover, there are always new forces that want to teach us to paint and they can be very powerful.

However, we can become aware of the racism that has been instilled in us. With this self-realization we can begin to change our own internalized prejudices and hate. Therefore, the road to racism does not have to be a dead end. Instead, it can be an eye-opening time of self-awareness in which we acknowledge the painter within all of us, and then commit to learning how to put the paintbrush down.

In these first two chapters, we have demonstrated how major institutions of society teach racism. Families, schools, the media, peer groups, law enforcement, and public settings are breeding grounds for learning to paint. In this next chapter, we will describe how painters are trained to not just paint indiscriminately but to paint particular differences.

## STUDENT TESTIMONIALS

*Voices of Pain and Voices of Hope* is more than a book; it is an instrumental tool that has helped transform my understanding of racism from a sort of abstract, philosophical and intellectual exercise to a very real and personal issue. As a 38-year-old White male, the truth is I've had little to no direct exposure to the insidious nature of racism, never mind being a victim of such. This is due in part to the bubble of White privilege I've been cocooned by most of my life. The stories in *Voices* painted a very real and down-to-earth picture for me: unfortunately, racism not only takes place on a daily basis, but also profoundly affects the lives of people I care about. The students in *Voices* could very well be my classmates and my friends. Dr. Rabow's book is a natural extension of his teaching that reminds me, particularly as a White male, to just stop and listen to those telling their personal stories, consciously suspending judgment. Understanding how someone feels and how they are affected is what ultimately counts, not whether I "believe" it or not, a luxury afforded to those of us in the "dominant class" and something I now willing and gladly forfeit. In my life, I love humor, and yet I cannot remember the last time I laughed at or told a joke based on racial or ethnic stereotypes since taking Dr. Rabow's class and reading his book, and that's a good thing and certainly a good start. *Voices* have helped to deflate my bubble of White privilege, replacing my ignorance with awareness and understanding.

> **Leonard Berkowitz, White, Male, 2003 California State, Northridge Graduate, Kinesiology Major, Physician Assistant Masters Student, Arizona School of Health Sciences**

It was after reading this book that I began to see the pain that I had caused others, directly and indirectly. I had started to develop weapons against racism, and this book was a welcome addition to my repertoire. *Voices of Pain and Voices of Hope* has been instrumental in assisting my struggle. The power that I see in *Voices* comes from its ability to demand action from its reader. I was not spoon fed the methodology to eradicate racism. Instead I found myself facing powerful and poignant questions about myself and the company I keep.

> **Aaron L. King, Black, Male, Psychology Major, California State University, Northridge**

Before I read *Voices of Pain and Voices of Hope* I felt ashamed of myself and of my family. I was never able to talk about my experiences with racism with anyone other than my immediate family because I felt ashamed that I had experienced such a thing. I didn't want my friends to know how my family and I have been treated. I thought that it was my fault. I thought it was my family's fault. I thought I deserved to be treated as if I were inferior. I have felt the effects of racism in schools, in the workplace, in public places, at restaurants, and at shopping stores. It feels bad. *Voices* has impacted my life in such a positive way. After reading all the stories in the book I realize that I am not alone. I realize that it is not my fault for being treated badly by racists. Racists want me to feel alone and ashamed of myself so that I don't speak up and defend myself. Racists want me to doubt myself so that they can keep taking advantage of me. And after reading *Voices,* I have gained a strength I never had. I no longer make myself feel like a victim. Now I speak up for myself and I don't feel ashamed of my culture or myself.

> **Dina Melendez, Salvadoran, Female, Student, California State University, Northridge**

*Voices of Pain and Voices of Hope* both comforted me and upset me. It enabled me to come to grips with stereotypes I had and to identify ones I saw around me. By reading about other people's experiences and reflecting on my own, I felt enlightened and empowered. I gained a support system and developed more than empathy as I began cultivating a strong voice and the desire to act.

I am now a teacher in a low-income, minority school. Rereading *Voices* has helped me to improve my practice and further my mission of equity and democracy in the classroom.

**Dominique Revel, White, Female, Graduate, University of California, Los Angeles, Teacher**

# The Strokes of Difference

Once children learn to paint and become adept with the paintbrush, what strokes do they make? Our students indicated that, as painters, they take aim at all that is different. Families, peers, and many others instruct painters to respond to the differences that distinguish themselves from subordinates. In this chapter, we examine the ways in which subordinate differences are selected, evaluated, and painted by dominants. It is this difference that is equated as "less than" in the painter's eyes, heart, and mind. It is this difference that often allows the painter to justify a canvas of racist ideologies and practices.[1]

## I. YOU'RE DIFFERENT!

The power of the paintbrush lies in its ability to paint difference as wrong. It's like laying a coat of white paint over a wall. When you lay white paint on a wall that is already white, the paint goes on easily. After one coat, the wall is white and shiny. However, when you paint white on top of another color, the old color shows through the white. And if the color is dark enough, it will show through several layers of white paint. Suddenly two walls, which seemed equal enough in the first place, are radically different. One stands out white and new. The other still looks different. This difference will require a lot of work to make it as white as the first wall.

Our metaphoric white paintbrush works on people in much the same way as it does on walls. It carries standards of Whiteness: skin colors, facial features, language, accents, and body types. When it passes over White

---

[1]Edward E. Sampson (1999) gives an excellent description of categorization and the way in which items may be assimilated or differentiated. When items fall within a category, they will be perceived and evaluated as more alike than they may actually be. This is the process of assimilation. When items fall into different categories, their differences are exaggerated and so they may be perceived as more different then they may actually be.

**47**

people, it glides on easily. However, when it passes over people of color, their differences still show through. These differences become obvious and problematic. The paintbrush determines who fits in and who doesn't. Because whiteness is the standard to which we are all held, people who are different are marked as inferior. Dominants frequently treat the skin of people of color as something that is undesirable, unattractive, and ugly. Over and over, students write about remembering how their skin color was treated as different. The paintbrush seeks out this difference, identifies it as ugly and inferior. Students remember where, when, and how the strokes of Whiteness were buried deeply into their awareness, poisoning their possibilities for self-love.

> The majority of my friends were Latinos, mainly from Mexico, and I was the "White washed" as silly as that sounds. Being "White" was being superior or classy or educated—to them, at least. I felt that I had the best of both worlds: I was perceived as "White" but I was also able to share a rich culture with people from so many different lands. Although when I was told I was "White washed" it was supposed to be negative, I felt it to be something positive—a compliment almost. "Being White" meant being educated, wealthy, and intelligent, not to mention snobby and bitchy. I didn't mind this "title." I aided them in painting me by buying into what "being White" meant. (Latina, female)

Because white skin color is the norm, it must be better and non-White skin color must be inferior.

## A. You're Different—Your Skin Color Isn't White So You're Inferior

Because race is so salient in our country, the paintbrush actively searches for the racial identity of subordinates. This is done most easily and frequently when children are young and skin color becomes noticeable. A Chicano male relates how he was forced to focus on his skin color. He also describes the pain and hatred he developed toward himself and others.

> I have been scarred by all these differences or should I say my culture! Many of the students [in class] spoke of the way they looked at themselves in the mirror and how they probed their features, hoping to sculpture them into the ideal. This brought back a vivid image of myself when I was in front of the mirror hoping to shed my skin because it was too dark. Why did I not accept my darkness? I guess I have always known. Not until this class have I really looked at the reasons behind it. My darkness made me feel different. In the middle of playing or talking to a classmate I would get asked, "Why are you so dark?"

"You're dark!" As if I had an explanation for this. Now I have scientific and geographical explanations, but that's not what they were looking for. They were looking to make me feel different, not to be seen as them. With that came the pain and hatred towards them and myself. (Latino, male)

The "innocence" of children reveals the power of the paintbrush. White children are rarely asked about their skin color; it is usually assumed to be "normal." Being a different color is constant in young children of color's lives, even to the point of internalization and self-hatred.

In the following example, a Latina described her family's positive response to her fair complexion. It appears that even her own family has succumbed to the dominant ideology: Whiteness is superior and preferred.

One of the biggest prejudices that I learned from my family as a child was the notion that people of color were somehow inferior to people of white or fair complexion. I never questioned this concept for I was very fair in complexion. Everyone in my family was very fair and some of us had green eyes, which made the remarks more believable at age 7. I remember my parents telling me, "you're so pretty because you're White." I never quite understood what they meant by the statement, till years later. The notion that Whites were more beautiful and smarter was ingrained into my mind and myself. All this learning was taking place in the comfort of my own home. In the eyes of my parents, you had to be fair in complexion to be accepted or beautiful. My aunts and uncles have similar views except that their offspring were darker in complexion. Their children would always get compared to me, "Why can't you be more like B, she is so nice and smart." The constant remarks and comments I heard in my living room became my truth. I trusted my parents, my aunts, and my uncles. I figured that maybe there was some truth to what they were saying. They had power and authority over me and so I mimicked their actions and attitudes. Similarly, I began to relate beauty and smartness to skin color. However, I never saw or considered myself as racist. I imagined everyone thought the same way my parents and I did. (Latina, female)

White is not just a skin color, but translates into a measure of beauty and intelligence. While the brush seeks to paint non-White skin because it is different, the paint penetrates deep beneath the skin. The effects of being painted are illustrated in the following excerpt. A woman's hatred for her skin color reveals a degree of self-loathing that is palpable. This Black woman cannot see anything beautiful or attractive about her dark skin. Any other color would be preferable to her.

As I grew up, I began to hate being dark. I thought, this is not who I am. I hated it. I'm brown not black. In school I used to always emphasize that my color was not like the crayon black, but like the crayon brown or sienna, anything but black. Once I colored a self-portrait of myself orange because the brown crayon was gone, anything but black, even purple would have sufficed. (African American, female)

Students of color are constantly being bombarded with the message of White-skin superiority. This image is so pervasive that many of the students of color reported an internalized sense of inferiority, shame, and self-loathing. The need to challenge this internalized view of White superiority prompted the slogan "Black is Beautiful," which developed in the 1960s as a way of declaring that the paint brush was wrong. It challenged the dominants' views of IQ tests, equal opportunity, and equality in education. It challenged the brush's standards for evaluating clothing, dress, and speech. It was a political statement and helped organize collective sentiments of pride and action. But slogans may not be strong enough to erase damaged aspirations and self-esteem. Slogans may not be able to overcome the constant, daily attacks on skin color. In the following excerpt, a Black woman describes her reaction to this political slogan. She expresses self-loathing and describes how her feelings about her skin color caused her to believe that Black people were anything but beautiful. This shame of Blackness penetrated so deeply that the young girl's isolation caused her to wish for a total change of racial identity.

I didn't think that Black was beautiful. I thought it was ugly, full lips, Gheri Curls, kinky hair that won't fall straight, everything. I thought all that was White was pretty and because I looked different, I was ugly. So when I look at my face in the mirror and see what I attribute to be Black features becoming more prominent, I would get upset and think, please don't let me look ugly like those girls. It took me a long time to get comfortable with my Blackness.

I remember that when I was younger, I wanted to be White. Not necessarily a White person, but I wanted to have white skin and straight hair. That was a very painful time for me. It was so hard to look in the mirror and wish to see something other than my own reflection. I never really questioned this desire that I had, but I knew to keep it a secret. I knew that I shouldn't let anyone know about how I felt about myself, and most importantly my family. When I think about why I wanted so badly to have white skin and straight hair, I remember instantly my experience at a predominantly White private school. I was never teased for being an African American and no one ever called my attention to that fact, but it manifested in the form of exclusion. For the first year or so, I didn't have any friends or anyone really to play with on an everyday basis. I never went to school expecting to play with any one child in particular. My memories are of being alone, reading and sewing and observing the things around me. Whenever we would play tag games, no one wanted to catch me. It was kind of like, oh she's it. I didn't let that get me down though . . . not as much as my desire to be White got me down. It was bad. I had this white shawl and I would put it on my head and pretend like it was long hair—shaking it and flinging that stupid thing everywhere, I hate to even remember that. In my dreams I was a pretty White girl discovering love with a White boy, I still remember his name. I would look at television and commercials and imagine that I was the cute little White girl on the screen. I would look through *Seventeen* magazines and identify characteristics that I wanted to possess. I would circle the picture and pray to God and wish on the stars that someday I would wake up and suddenly . . . I hate to even think about that . . . No, this feeling of guilt is from wanting to be White, and why did I want to be White? I felt excluded, unloved, and unhappy in my world. Inclusion, love, and happiness were portrayed only in the lives of White people. "Leave it to Beaver," "The Brady Bunch," the commercials, the movies, the magazines was the White world. I was in the Black world. My people were on the evening news, in still pictures showing their faces and their profiles. My people were the robbers and rapists in the movies. My people were in the ghettos and the slums. Whenever I saw my people outside of my limited environment, they looked like I felt, unloved, unhappy, excluded. So who am I mad at? White society, the European culture, for portraying my people as they would like to see them. (African American, female)

Skin color is only the beginning of the White painters' attacks on difference. Being White and judging others who don't conform to a White standard involves much more than just skin color.

# B. Your Other Physical Characteristics Also Indicate Your Inferiority

If only skin color was painted, lighter skinned people of color could "pass." This would be dangerous to the dominants' set of beliefs and practices. Passing would mean that some non-Whites could fully be representative of American life. This would in turn affect our definition of what it means to be American. The opportunity for all people of color to be validated is too threatening for dominants. If skin color was not treated as "less," then the norm of Whiteness as being more beautiful, more intelligent, or more motivated would be challenged and indeed eradicated. However, skin color is not the only difference selected by the brush. A non-White appearance is attacked on a number of dimensions. In the following example, a Filipino male is belittled and denigrated for both language and eye shape by his neighborhood peers.

When I was about 8 years old, I was walking up my street to play with some kids around the block. There were two kids who were walking towards me. As I was walked past them, they both squinted their eyes with their fingers and in a voice, loud enough for me to hear, mimicked an Asian language in a degrading way. While they were doing this, I thought to my-self they couldn't be doing this to me. I never felt that I looked Chinese or Japanese, so I turned around and looked to see if they could've been teas-ing someone else, but there wasn't anyone else around. I remember that my first thoughts were not anger towards the boys, but angry at getting teased and confused for another Asian. This is the beginning of many experiences that have made me internalize oppression about my race (Filipino), as well as the Asian race. (Filipino, male)

Like skin color, this young man's eyes were not only depicted as dif-ferent but as strange and ugly. By looking around him and seeing the dom-inance of "Whiteness" and White features, this young man accepted this evaluation. Rather than learning pride in his appearance and his ethnicity, he turned his anger on himself. And rather than hating the people who be-littled him he learned to hate members of his own group.

In the next excerpt, a Filipino female indicates how "Westernized" fea-tures of Whiteness were emphasized in her culture. As this Filipina found, sometimes one's own parents wield the brush.

Growing up, I was taught that the more "White" you looked, the prettier you were. If your nose was sharp, if your skin was light, if your eyes were more rounded, you were praised for having such characteristics. I grew up with this mentality that dark was ugly, or just not as socially accepted by my family and relatives. (Even though most Filipinos have darker skin, the ones who were lighter were deemed beautiful.) I remember telling my girl-friends that I would want to marry a guy who was White because my kids would be beautiful. This is an example of the self-hate that is found in var-ious cultures. I find myself not appreciating the beauty of my own culture, the beauty of my own unique features. It's terrible how my culture has suc-cumbed to deeming "White" as beautiful. Even after the cruelty Filipinos have endured, especially when Filipinos first migrated here. In my Filipino American experience class I learned of the hatred and discrimination Fil-ipinos had suffered. And it made me angry when my mom praised my cousin for having more Westernized features. It's like we try to downplay our own beautiful, natural features. (Filipino, female)

In the next excerpt, a Latina discusses how her parents did not accept her hair and eye color and how they, unknowingly, reinforced the White painters' standards of beauty.

When I was in second grade, I joined our local swim team. I went swim-ming every day and because of the chlorine, my hair would turn light. On top of the chlorine, my mother put Sun-In in my hair to lighten it as well. What kinds of messages were being sent to me through this? By the time I got to high school, I was putting Sun-In in my own hair and eventually dyed it. My hair was basically blond, and my mother kept telling me how much she loved my hair color and how she wanted me to keep it light. Later, as I got older and I needed glasses, I got contact lenses. I remember coming home from my optometrist saying, "Dad, I'm getting contacts." The first thing out of his mouth was, you should get colored lenses, and he wanted me to get blue contacts. So, not only did he love my hair light, he wanted me to look even whiter. Even today, I sometimes feel as though I favor blond hair and light eyes as my idea of beauty. (Mexican American, female)

Another Latina learns from her mother and aunt that White features are superior. She also describes how she internalized these standards of beauty to the point where she hated herself, her culture, and eventually her own family.

I learned to hate darker skin and I think that that is perhaps part of the reason behind me having an adolescence full of timidness and shame in my culture, my appearance, and my family. I hated being Mexican, dark, short, and having brown eyes. This self-hatred was heightened during this point of life. I learned to feed into what my family believed was and was not. I remember how I hated those "beaners," those "indios" as my mother called them. Saddest in all this, was that my mother was dark in skin tone, was short, and had brown eyes. I grew ashamed of her too. The seeds had been planted so deeply now that they allowed me to hate my family. (Latina, female)

Body image is a very key aspect of a young person's developing identity. In the following excerpt, a Latina describes her experiences with her ethnic body type.

Although skin color never really was an issue for me because my peers admired my ability to tan so easily, my body type was an issue. My basic body shape, which would later find some affirmation by women and men of my own ethnic background, was not the norm amongst the White women who were my peers. Tall and slender was the ideal. Knowing this and seeing the preference for this type definitely gave me a sense of being unattractive. As a young woman I was very uncomfortable in my own skin. Struggling with my body image has been a long and difficult and very personal struggle. It took a long time to change this. It wasn't until I moved to California that I was able to overcome my deep sense of being undesirable. Once I moved to California and saw other young women I wondered what my self-concept would have been like if I had grown up with other young women who would have been more like me or if the media had affirmed my looks. (Latina, female)

Sometimes, the focus on one's "defects" can lead the painted person to obsess about being different. In the following excerpt, a Black woman yearns for a different eye color. Her hope was, and still is, that this would make a difference in her life and would bring her greater adoration.

I have always wanted a different eye color. Now I can see where that is coming from because when society looks at a person, the eye color and the skin are examined first. No one ever comes up to me and says "gosh, your eyes are so beautiful" because they are just brown. But I often compliment people with beautiful green or hazel eyes and I begin to picture myself with those same eyes. I know guys who love black women with green, blue or even hazel eyes, just as long as they are not brown. Because of this I still want an eye color other than brown. This is what I have come to realize as my internalized oppression to be something that I am not. I think that as a light-skinned Black woman, most Black men already accept me, but if I had green eyes I would be even more adored. (African American, female)

Similarly, this Arab male wonders how a White appearance might affect other areas of his life.

I remember staring at the male models in the pages of magazines like G.Q., and wondering how different my life would be if I had their features. Maybe then I could command the respect from White America I felt I deserved. I felt that the good looking White boys in junior high not only got the best looking girlfriends, but they were given way more respect, positive feedback, and encouragement from students and faculty than I. I always thought that I was smarter and funnier than all of them and therefore I should have been the recipient of such praise, but that didn't happen. (Arab, male)

Trying to measure up to dominants' vision of Whiteness, subordinates often fantasize how other aspects of their lives might be different if they looked more White. Wishing to be lighter skinned and possess "Whiter" features, caused many of the students to wonder about how their non-White appearance has affected their personal relationships, education and job opportunities.

Sometimes I wish I was a little lighter, or that my hair was not so dark. I wish I had finer features. It would be pretty nice to experience some of that White privilege. Sometimes I envy my roommate because she looks white. I honestly believe that she is able to get away with a lot because of the way she looks. I often wonder how my life would differ if I looked White. Would I have more opportunities? Would I have been put in seventh grade algebra class if I looked White? Would I have gotten a different job? I do not know. But I think my life would be a little different. I know that I would be treated differently by some people. (Mexican American, female)

The brush also asserts standards for male attractiveness. In the following excerpt, a Chicano man describes his anguish about his skin, speech, and desire to be less brown.

Now that I look back, high school and junior high school was a time when I wanted to be White. I see how many of the things I did were ways of trying to live up to a societal expectation of beauty. For example, I always wanted my hair to be lighter and curly. So, in junior high, I got a perm. It was one of the most horrendous haircuts in the history of mankind. Yet, I did not learn my lesson. I continued to believe a perm looked good on me until I came to UCLA. For a couple of years in my life, I wish I had been born less brown. (Chicano, male)

Pervasive self-hatred is often accompanied by a wish to be free of pain and self-hate. This wish is often transformed into a longing to be White. The hope is that if one is White, it will bring relief from the pain. In the following excerpt, a Mexican man describes how he felt "good" when called White, a feeling that he had never had when he thought of himself as Mexican.

I eventually got a job with the company and was getting along with all the workers. On our daily trips to the sites I would always have conversations with my boss and other colleagues. One day my boss said that I was not Mexican, that I was White. I felt good that day. I felt that I was someone in this country of ours. After years of being called a wetback or Mexican, it felt good to be called White. (Mexican, male)

For this young man, having a dominant strip him of his heritage and background felt like a compliment.

## C. Your Names Don't Sound Right: Another Indication of Inferiority

The paintbrush does not only identify physical features that set subordinates apart from dominants, it also recognizes and looks down upon accents, different types of foods, and ethnic names. When children with different skin colors and physical features come under the brush strokes, they often want to change their appearance. When other racial and ethnic markers come under attack, subordinates often find themselves wanting to change these, too—even if the change means denying their heritage and giving up part of their identity.

It is very common for children with ethnic names to pick up "American" nicknames. It is also common for dominants to suggest or even insist that a subordinate be referred to by a nickname. Many dominants don't want to go through the trouble of learning to pronounce a foreign sounding name.

In the following excerpt an Armenian woman describes how for many years teachers "butchered" her name. Although she acted politely, her anger was always there under the surface. On the day of her graduation, the teacher once again ignored her name. She now lives with a fantasy of what she would have said.

My name is very long and difficult to pronounce. All throughout my education in the United States, I have received comments on how hard my name looks. I had gotten accustomed to it in high school, but the whole ordeal always made me feel like a foreigner. I would tell my new teachers not to worry, that I understood if they butchered my name, but I was only being nice about it. I did not want to rock the boat. Although I had suppressed the anger I felt at my name always being ridiculed, I never said anything at all. The ultimate example is my graduation from the Law and Government Magnet School. My counselor of 4 years was calling out the names of graduates, and when she reached my name, she said, "I'm not even going to try." She only said my first name. I approached the podium, received my certificate and felt completely insulted and angry. Four years of hard work, 4 years of showing constant respect to this woman, and she could not even attempt to say my full name at my own graduation. After that day, I always had fantasies of having caused a scene. If I could live it all over again, I would grab the microphone and say that I think she should try, I would say, "She should at least try folks, wouldn't you all like to hear Mrs. F. try to say my name?" (Armenian, female)

Dominants often select and assign a new name for the subordinate. Dominants do not give a great deal of attention in selecting a name. They rarely think about what they are doing because they believe they are simply changing someone's name. But a name is who you are. Your family gave it to you. It is yours alone. When you change someone's name from Jose to Joe, from Eliazare to Elly, Yuseph to Joe, Zalika to "Z", LaShell to Shelley, Trang to Tina, Ijeoma to Ida, or Paulino to Paul, you rob them of a piece of their identity.

In the following example, a Latino has a name that is unique and highly valued. He describes the reactions from his peers and his boss who continually mispronounce his name. He feels they're taking away his uniqueness. Eventually he grows angry and tired of having to teach dominants.

Growing up, I was ashamed of my name because it is not very common in the United States or in Latin America. My name is Blas, its Vasque—a region in northern Spain. Not only is my name special to me because it's unique, but it also has sentimental value. This name belonged to my paternal grandfather who passed away before I was born. However, because my peers teased me, I chose to go by my middle name, Humberto. Even then, my peers were not satisfied and continued to mispronounce my name incorrectly. Despite my effort to acculturate, I was unable to satisfy anyone. I recall when I got my first job; my boss changed my name from Humberto to Bert without my permission. He claimed it sounded better and was easier to pronounce. It really pissed me off but I stayed quiet. As time progressed, I got tired of not being acknowledged and tired of justifying who I was. (Latino, male)[2]

---

[2]This student felt that the reader could benefit only if his real name was included in the excerpt.

A Mexican American male discusses his efforts to make it easier on Whites who struggle with his name.

I went through a time in which I wanted to be White due to the fact that I wanted to be accepted with the other White kids. Nevertheless, as I look at it now I realize how close I came to becoming one of those "White washed" individuals who never discloses his or her own *raza* (people). I also fell into the role in which White people put me in, for example, my name is Roberto, not Rob, Bob, or Bobby. I never corrected anyone about calling me something different than Roberto because of respect and because I just felt that many teachers had a hard time rolling the "R" in Roberto. Even today, many people who do not roll the "R's" will still call me Robert, but those who try to say Roberto and do not roll their "R's" will get more respect from me than those who either do not try or whom I have already corrected. (Mexican American, male)

Those who wield the paintbrush can also make children suffer by merely mispronouncing their names. In the following excerpt, an Arab student's patience with helping and correcting others pronounce his name has worn thin, and prompted him to adopt an "American" name, thus yielding a part of his identity.

One painful memory that will stick with me forever is that I did not correct people (students, teachers, etc.) for incorrectly pronouncing my name, and even allowing them to give me a nickname to make it easier for them. The most painful memory I have is one time I was making a collect call home for a ride, and remembering all the horrible experiences I had with the phone operators. They would ask for my name to accept the call and then would say stupid things like, "What did you say your name was?" or just repeat something that sounded nothing like my name. I decided just to say my name was Mark and speak up when a family member answered the phone. However, my father answered the phone and would not accept a call from a Mark, even when I was talking over the operator saying it was me. I called back and got the ride. On the way home, I felt like my father was disgusted with me. He said that I needed to be proud, to force people to deal with my culture and me. (Arab, male)

This student worked to make life easier for Whites by giving up part of his identity and offending his father.

A Filipina student, from an early age, learned to hate her last name because of her teachers' insensitivity and ignorance.

In grade school, I always hated when a new teacher or substitute would wrongly pronounce my last name whenever it was time to call attendance. I distinctly remember a third grade substitute asking me with a look of impatience and disgust after wrongly pronouncing my name, "so are you Chinese, Korean, Oriental, Japanese?" When I told him I was Filipino, he just looked at me and said, "what is that??!!" I just felt so embarrassed in front of the whole class. From this point on, I remember wishing I had an American last name, just so that I could fit in, just so that people wouldn't look at me as though I was an alien. I hated being different! (Filipina, female)

Dominants, of course, have a language that is seen as superior. Their names for their own children are "normal," easy to learn and pronounce. Mispronouncing the names of subordinates or changing them to a more convenient nickname is often demeaning to students of color. In the following excerpt, we hear how a young Latina despises her last name because of the racial associations made by painters.

My sister looks completely White and does not speak a word of Spanish, but she has a Mexican last name: Gutierrez. One day we were driving and out of the blue she said, "I want to change my name. I hate it. I can't stand it when people see my name and assume I speak Spanish, because I don't! It makes me so mad." I was extremely shocked and felt myself getting ready to yell at her. What the hell was she saying? There was so much anger in her voice, but where did it come from? All at once I felt a flood of emotions rush through my veins. Her words cut deeply into my heart. I was ashamed that she would disrespect our grandfather and the generations before him. Yet I also wanted to hug her and tell her that I was sorry for all the times she was ever ridiculed for not being able to communicate in Spanish. I knew how she felt. I, too, had resented Latinos telling me that I should be speaking my "native" language. Excuse me? These people had no idea who we were and knew nothing about our background or family. They just had to take the opportunity to belittle someone by judging us. (Mexican American, female)

## II. IMITATING THE DOMINANTS

We recognize that subordinates also use and practice prejudice, racism, and stereotypes. Why would this happen? What causes subordinates to paint other subordinates? We believe that one of the reasons that subordinates paint other subordinates is because they have often been caught up in the dominants' message of White superiority. Racism occurs in all institutions (political, economic, education, and religion) and at all levels of society (cultural, social and psychological). This constant participation and exposure to prejudice teaches us and prompts us all to be racist. In other words if Latinos are continually exposed to dominant stereotypes about African Americans as lazy and if Asians are exposed to stereotypes about Arabs as terrorists, they will often adopt the views of the dominant painters without recognizing that they did just that. Although some members of subordinate groups can resist dominant messages, the impact of daily living, shopping, and working takes its toll on all of us. Thus, subordinates often enact prejudice on other subordinates.

First, we do not believe that prejudice from a subordinate, such as a female, is in any way equivalent to the prejudice of a dominant male. Specifically, the impact of dominant racism is much more potent than its subordinate counterpart. For example, when we ask whose oppression has greater consequences, in terms of gender, we see that men are advantaged and that they benefit from their prejudice. We see that women are underrepresented at all the higher levels of business, education, and government. Women's wages continue to be lower than men's despite equal work. So, the oppression of those with greater power (dominants) is far more consequential than the painting of subordinates to other subordinates.

A second reason that subordinates become painters can be explained by the universal tendency to want to increase one's value at the expense of others. If one subordinate group practices racism against another group, the former increases its own sense of empowerment and entitlement to maintain its hierarchical place. In doing so, the oppressive subordinate group imitates dominants in their practices of racism. Not surprisingly, dominants often encourage this imitation. This lack of unity between subordinates serves to empower dominants.

In the next example, a Mexican American woman remembers making fun of immigrant men who were field workers.

> I can remember when I was about 8 years old, my family would drive past places where men were out in the fields working. I had forgotten about this, but I recall my cousin jokingly yelling out the window "La Migra, La Migra." At the time, I thought it was the funniest thing, we would laugh hysterically thinking that all the men would stop what they were doing and run and hide. Gosh, I can't believe we used to do that. Granted we were just kids with no clue, but did we ever think about what we were doing? Or if they could hear us, how it made them feel? And what about our parents, why didn't they say anything? (Mexican American, female)

As she recalls this experience, this student realizes that what she and her cousin were doing was hurtful, and that the fun they had was at others' expense. This quote also demonstrates how children of color teach each other how to paint like dominants. Just as Whites make ethnic jokes to show their superiority, subordinates often find ways to laugh at those who they feel are inferior to them. The paintbrush is handed down and thrives from one racial group to another.

The reader who is not a person of color can probably imagine a time in their lives when peers and parents and teachers ridiculed them. They were called names, or told they were too fat, too short, too skinny, four-eyed, nerdy, and the like. The pain that accompanies those slurs is certainly similar to the pain felt by the students you have been reading about. The difference in the name calling that White children experience is that it is not institutionalized as a regular, ongoing form of discrimination. Also, the prejudicial slurs insult the individual and not their whole culture, family, or history. People who are not athletic somehow seem to get promoted despite their athletic inadequacy. For the students of color that you have been reading about, the names, the slurs, the innuendoes are repetitive and can often occur on a daily basis. The oppression is much more significant, not necessarily in its pain, but its consequence.

In sum, what the white paintbrush establishes for children of color is that their skin, facial features, and their names are peculiar and their hair and body type are ugly and unattractive; their social identity is undesirable. They are oh-so different. But in a very surprising twist, the paintbrush turns around and works to "lump" all subordinates together—they are also painted as the same. So with the messages of undesired and undesirable differences, now come the other messages about subordinates being all the same: similar intelligence, similar ambitions, similar character, and a similar future and place in the world. In this chapter, we showed how subordinates are painted and made to feel that their differences are what makes them inferior to dominants. In our next chapter, we will demonstrate to the reader how subordinates are lumped together and treated as the same by dominant painters. In this way, dominants ignore differences between and among subordinates. So on the one hand, the differences of subordinates are emphasized, and on the other, the differences are ignored.

## STUDENT TESTIMONIALS

Having grown up White I always had the privilege of never having to realize my own racial identity, or never being forced to attribute much of my identity (i.e., status, achievements, economic advancement) to my race. Upon reading *Voices* I became aware of that privilege, and more importantly I became aware of the lack of that privilege in the other races around me. I always knew that we define ourselves by our race, but I never knew to what extent or for what reasons. With the progress of racial identity I gained from *Voices* I was able to see in the immediate world around me that race is a very real thing, and to some people it is the most significant thing they have. Personally, the book stood as a sort of wake-up call. It let me know that where we are today, in terms of civil rights, is no further than where we were 40 years ago. In fact, the latency of today's racism, as proved repeatedly in *Voices,* is something that is harder to pinpoint and therefore harder to confront. With the stories that *Voices* provided, it gave me a clear view of the mechanics of modern racism, and as such a way to approach it. So as a White male, it not only concretely proved what I had always suspected, but it more importantly showed me that if ever there was time that anyone should become active in race relations and equality in America it is now. So now when I see something to be racist, I have the ability to do something about it, as opposed to just saying something about it.

> **John Hess, White, Male, Student, California State University Northridge**

It was a great awakening for me to read the stories of victimization that happened to my peers and colleagues. I had no clue that in 2003, people my age experienced this degree of racism and prejudice. I was especially shocked to learn how Asians feel they are viewed by American culture. I now see that I have some responsibility for understanding my own prejudices and that I need to open myself to this idea and to talk to others about it.

> **Amy Johnstone, White, Female, Student, California State University, Northridge, Future Teacher**

*Voices of Pain and Voices of Hope* was both a wake-up call and a reality check that told me a very simple message. Racism is alive and well today. It is not uncommon for many people to assume that race is no longer a factor in social interactions and social institutions. It is. The experiences of my peers and the voices in this book have made me more sensitive and aware of the diversity of experiences that people go through. It taught me that race is always an active part of one's identity, regardless of class or privilege. Also, because I too was able to share my experiences, it gave me a sense of shared experience, the feeling that I was not alone. My notions of racism, racial identity, and the hope for racial harmony were challenged, altered, and questioned, all at the same time. Dr. Rabow's class and the voices in this book was a landmark for my development as a human being and my sensitivity and understanding of race.

> **Jeremy Lalas, Filipino American, Male, Cum Laude, UCLA 2004, B.A. Sociology**

*Voices of Pain and Voices of Hope* is an intriguing and brutally honest depiction of discrimination in the lives of everyday people. What makes this book so effective is that it gives honest accounts of events that really happen in people's lives. It is easy to teach about racism from a strictly academic standpoint, but this type of pedagogy simply defines the problem instead of offering solutions. I personally can relate to the painful stories in this book because I have gone through similar experiences. When people are given the opportunity to experience other people's hardships through reading their personal stories, it is much easier to understand the harsh realities of American society. Statistics can only provide people with a general idea or glimpse into the concept of discrimination, while learning about other people creates the opportunity for one to feel bad and inevitably want to make a change. I cringed at some of the stories that were told in this book, but the anger that is created by reading these stories has been transformed into positive motivation for me to make a difference in the world through my actions as well as my speech.

**David Laster, African American, Male, Student, California State University, Northridge**

As a White person experiencing life from a dominant perspective I had grown up thinking that more or less we all play on a level playing field. Of course I understood that there were occurrences of prejudice but I thought these to be the exception rather than the rule, at least on the coasts. This book, *Voices of Pain and Voices of Hope* has allowed me to see into places that my own world could not otherwise take me. I was able to read about the experiences of his students and feel their pain and outrage. I was able to learn that these horrible experiences are still occurring on a daily basis and I was able to see that through speaking out when I see even what seems to be small intolerances or "jokes" that I can help to change attitudes of what is acceptable. This book helps us all learn, through others' eyes, the injustices that we cannot see living in our own small sphere of existence and gives us concrete proof that we must stand up and speak out against intolerance.

**Samantha Seegull, White, Female, Student, California State University, Northridge**

# IV

## The Strokes of Sameness

The previous chapter revealed how the paintbrush highlights differences and then uses these differences to demean and humiliate subordinates. In this chapter, we will show how generalizations and prejudgments of subordinates as being all the same are equally as damaging and degrading. Evaluating subordinates as the "same" includes grouping them together by character, intelligence, morality, and/or ambition. As the paintbrush points out subordinates as different from dominants, it also works to make sure that they are defined as less. This lumping ignores their uniqueness, talents, and potential, and makes success more difficult for subordinates.

Richard Pryor in his 1977 album, *Who Me? I'm Not Him,* describes this phenomenon. Kids are different; some like baseball, others like swimming. Some like reading and others like drawing. Children are unique and different. Pryor loved being a kid and then it all changed.

> *I like being a kid very much. I do . . . I really love it—'cause if you was a kid, you didn't have to be anything else. I was a kid until I was about eight . . . then I became a Negro.*

In this quip, Pryor describes the "grouping and lumping" phenomenon. He suggests that White children are just children: their racial category leaves them unmarked, but being a Black child sets you apart. The unmarked are differentiated from each other based on their uniqueness. We all notice and comment upon what children do and accomplish. In contrast, sooner or later, subordinate children are grouped. They are not just children, but Black children, Latino/a children, Asian children, or Mexican children.

Even though there may be clear differences between peoples of color, members of each of the subordinate groups tend to be labeled as all the same. When we hear people say, "Why don't they just speak English?" we are hearing people who are frustrated that subordinates are not rushing to adopt their language and their standards. When we hear people say, "Why do they need their own day or month for history—why can't they just be content with regular American history?" we are hearing people who are frustrated that subordinates do not want to meekly accept a history that distorts their reality. When we hear people say, "Why can't they work hard like I did?" we are also hearing that minorities must be lazy and want something for nothing. Dominants are often frustrated when subordinates don't want to be just like them; they get upset when subordinates want to maintain their individuality and want to create new, alternative ways of life, or challenge the dominants' views of history and social justice. Most of all, dominants want to make sure that their views and ways remain the norm. This latter sentiment is achieved by purposefully ignoring all that is unique, original, or different about subordinates.

## I. YOU'RE THE SAME—I DON'T NEED TO KNOW YOU AS AN INDIVIDUAL

The paintbrush does more than highlight and pathologize people's differences, it also works to lump together all people who are different. In the United States, we celebrate individuality; we strive to be unique. But in many cases, it is the privilege of being dominant that allows people to be noticed. In the following excerpt, a Filipino reacts to the dominant's lumping of all Asians into one category.

> One of the biggest problems not addressed by the dominant society is that they lump Asians into one category. They say, that we all look alike, sound alike, and eat the same food. But they are wrong. It hurts to think that one cannot differentiate from another. (Filipino, male)

In the next example an Asian male describes the ways in which he is continually being painted either as a nerd, nonathletic, musically gifted, and thuggish. He is none of these.

> I have been treated differently because I am Asian and different than the White majority. Asians are stereotyped as being nonathletic, musical, and either nerdish or thuggish. Sadly, I have little to no musical ability, I slack off way too much, and I tend to be fairly athletic and aggressive when playing sports, and I do not fit into the nerd or thug roles. For some reason understanding of math or English never came easy as it did later. When I was 7, a guy in my class asked if he could study with me and I was happy to say yes. He didn't know me very well but he knew I was Asian and thus supposed to be intelligent. He assumed that I knew the answers as thus expected me to finish the work for both of us. He was disappointed as I was hoping he could help me with the problems. At this age I felt bad that I couldn't live up to people's expectations of me. At the same time, I felt pressured to fulfill the stereotype though I didn't know how I could. (Chinese, male)

The privilege of Whiteness allows dominants to be recognized for their individual qualities. The media is frequently guilty of slighting and ignoring persons who are not White and classifying them into a single category. In the following example, an Asian man describes his anger at the media's one-dimensional depiction of his murdered friend. The television reports simply referred to the deceased as "Asian" in striking contrast to how White victims were portrayed.

> The American media is biased. Two weeks ago, my friend T was brutally murdered. When reporters reported the story, none of them mentioned that he graduated from UCLA with honors and was waiting for an acceptance letter from medical schools. I was so upset when I didn't hear any description of my friend's achievement. I am upset because if this had happened to a White person, something positive would have been mentioned. For instance, two days ago a (White) couple jumped off a cliff. News reporters must have spent more time telling us how great these kids were (e.g. straight A's, or outgoing). I was infuriated when I realized that the same newscaster only spent a few seconds reporting my friend's murder. This reaffirmed my thought that the dominant society has not yet fully recognized Asian people. My friend needed to be recognized as an individual, as someone who had worked hard in school so that he could attend medical school, as an ex-president of the Vietnamese Student Association, as an inspiration for his friends. Instead, people who saw the news coverage of T will probably remember him as a product of the growing violence among the Asian community. Whatever it is that the public remembers him as, they won't remember him like they do the self-destructive White couple. (Vietnamese, male)

For dominants, Whiteness or race is neutral. The identities of Whites become tied to the subjects they major in, the sports they play, or the careers they choose. On the other hand, the identities of subordinates are submerged in the lumping process. When they are noticed assumptions are made about their personalities, their morality, and their behavior. When parents ask their daughter about her new boyfriend, they want to know what he looks like, how he treats her, what he's interested in. But often, if parents find out that the boyfriend is Black, that's enough information. They dislike him immediately, because of all the images that are conjured up by his skin color. Drawing on a nonrace example, when people find out that the day care worker is homosexual, they often yank their children out of preschool because they assume that all gay people are sexual deviants. In everyday life, the things that mark subordinates as "different" allow dominants to group them as all the same. It then becomes the subordinates' responsibility to prove that they are "exceptions."

# II. YOU'RE THE SAME—YOUR NAME DOESN'T MATTER

Naming someone is a very powerful experience. For instance, calling someone a "mom" evokes many more images than simply that of a woman who has given birth to a child. Similarly, people go to great pains to make sure that they are addressed by the proper title: judges are called "your honor," king and queens are referred to as "your Excellency." Just as these titles evoke images, the names that we give to racial categories similarly embody deep symbolism. While the word "mom" implies all kinds of emotions and "your honor" implies respect, racial names of subordinates carry with them ideas of intelligence, morality, ambition, talent, and immigrant status.

All people belong to some official racial category or categories. When White people do things, their race goes unmentioned, for instance, "a teacher was arrested for sexually harassing students" as opposed to "a young Black male stole a car." On the other hand, a range of names marks non-White races. By marking non-Whites with these names, the paintbrush highlights all subordinates as the same—and such sameness often translates into an image of deviance. Because of a history of exploitation, many terms for racial categories become *so* loaded that with just one word, the impact can be seared into the psyche of a child forever.

In the following example, an 8-year-old female is called a name that she implicitly knew was horrible and degrading despite never having heard it before. Up until the moment of being labeled, the young girl and her best friend are having a great time. The student's playfulness and friendliness is ignored as she is painted with a name.

> I can remember as a child having a good friend named J, who I did everything with. We were the best of friends. J was White and I was Black but that was never an issue. One day we were in her backyard playing in the snow. We were having a great time. I remember starting a snowball fight. Well, we were getting wet and cold from the snow and were ready to stop. I threw my last snowball and it hit J in the face. J became mad. All of a sudden she shouted, "Nigger" into my face. She kept repeating it. Soon her little brother and sister joined in. I started to cry. "Why were they saying this to me?" I felt so scared and helpless. I ran all the way home. That day I knew that I was different. (African American, female)

Names are not limited to Black children. Indeed all subordinates involuntarily join the ranks of the labeled. In the following excerpt, the terms used for a young Korean are incorrect but they nevertheless hurt her.

> As horribly blunt as children can be I heard insults such as "You little chink! Why don't you go back to your own country?!" and "You think

you're so smart you little nip!" hurled at me. Even the other Korean children would tease me because I seemed to look more Chinese than Korean. I can clearly remember numerous instances when I would come home crying and hating that I was Korean. (Korean, female)

This quote shows the power of labeling. By naming people and allowing their racial background to be the primary form of identification, these children were saying that all people who look Asian were the same.

In the next excerpt, a spray-painted word on a new house impresses upon this student that dominants will decide "who" he is just because they know his racial background. He learned that who he was must be undesirable. The fact that his family was highly educated, affluent, accomplished, or highly moral was irrelevant. Only race mattered to the painters.

I remember when I was 8, my grandmother's sister and her family moved to Arcadia, a predominantly White, middle-upper class neighborhood in 1982. When we went over to see her house, someone had graffitied with spray paint, "Fuck You Nip." I was so puzzled why anyone would write such a thing. I was even more confused, because the neighborhood looked so quiet and nice. I asked my mom if auntie and grandma's sister would be safe living here and I remember my mom saying, "I sure hope they will be." Her answer frightened me, but when she said this, I knew that I would have some tough battles ahead of me. (Korean, male)

In the next situation, a biracial (Japanese and White) female recalled her age, the year, the place, and the individuals who were involved when she was first subjected to a racial slur. This specificity suggests the "traumatic aspects" of the event.

I was 6 years old at the time, living with my mom and sister in Garden Grove, a city in Orange County. My elementary school had a diversity of students: Whites, Hispanics, and Asians. The majority of the Asians were Vietnamese. My White friends would call them "nips" or "gooks." I was even guilty of this myself. Even though I am half-Japanese, I did not look very Asian; not one of my White friends noticed that I was part Asian. One day after school my friend Jane came over and saw that my mom was Asian. She did not say anything at that time but I can still visualize the shock and surprise on her face when I introduced this little Japanese woman as my mother. The following day at school, she came up to me with a few of our other friends and said, "My daddy said that you are a 'nip' too because your mother is Asian." Shocked by what she had just said to me, I tried to defend myself by stupidly saying, "but my mom is Japanese, not Vietnamese." J followed with, "That doesn't matter because my daddy said that all them Asians are the same. They are all 'gooks'." I did not continue to argue with her because there was no point. I was so embarrassed because our other friends were just staring in disbelief. I was very angry and hurt—this big secret that I was withholding from all my friends had just been revealed and I was not prepared to really defend myself. I could not believe J would call me those same awful names that we called out to the Vietnamese students." (Biracial, Japanese White, female)

Often subordinates think they are dominants until forcefully reminded otherwise. Before the slur was applied to her, this student found it fun to call other children racial names. Clearly, to dominants, name-calling seems benign. It seems like a game, especially to young children. To subordinates, the name-calling and group labeling (which they face everywhere they go) deeply affects their self-image. Ongoing name-calling created difficulty for this young Middle Eastern male who was unable to focus on his education.

Sometimes I got called "mean Arab" and other such things, especially during times when the Middle East was heavily covered in the news. These children didn't know any better, it came naturally to them. I remember being occupied with worries about being different and inferior. There were many times I can remember not being able to think straight days after a confrontation. I was too worried about what the other children were thinking. For many years this worrying affected my performance in school no matter how hard I tried. (Arab, male)

Naming and grouping someone is an exercise of power. The power by dominants to rename and regroup subordinates is rarely done in a complimentary fashion. Racial names are derogatory and designed to make the other feel less worthy, less valued, less attractive, and less desirable. A name that others hold as something you "are" has an impact on the self. The name becomes part of the subordinate's identity, telling them of their sameness and that they should stay in their place.

## III. YOU'RE THE SAME—MY JOKES ARE "ALL IN GOOD FUN"

In addition to slurs, the paintbrush uses jokes to respond to, accentuate, and belittle subordinates. These jokes treat all members of ethnic, racial, and religious groups as similar. In fact, many of these jokes rely on shared stereotypes in order to be funny in the first place. These jokes are very difficult for young people to challenge. It's hard to stand up for yourself, especially when everyone else is laughing. The painter often believes his words to be funny, and as a dominant, may not realize that they reemphasize similarity and pain. In the following example, an Asian student recalled jokes aimed at her race. Even though she objected to the jokes, they deeply impacted her. She recalls one from high school and the other from college. Both jokes are equally painful for this student.

Setting: some time in high school, probably during junior or senior year

J: "How did Chinese people come up with their last names?"

L: (going along with it) "How?"

J: "When someone dropped the silverware down the stairs, it went ching chang-ching-chang-etc."

L: "F-you!" (not too serious, but not too facetiously either)

J: (laughing)

Setting: about 2–3 years ago while I was either 18 or 19 years old. I was having lunch on campus with my White roommate.

J: "Why do Chinese men walk with their hands behind their backs?"

L: (with a reluctant look on her face like she's thinking to herself) "Why are you saying this to me?"

J: "To protect their wallets, get it?"

L: (just looks at Jennifer, upset and unamused.)

J: "Oh relax! Don't get all sensitive!"

It was from this last joke that I first learned of the stereotype that all Chinese people were considered cheap and "protective" of their money. The jokes were painful, but I usually left such remarks alone. Besides a look of upset or disapproval, I never pursued the issue with J. It would have been difficult to talk to her about it, and I always felt that she would be too stubborn to own up to it. (Chinese American, female)

Even for adults, it can be very difficult to challenge racist jokes, especially if they are directed at your own group. In this next example, a Vietnamese woman described a dinner with her boyfriend's family who proceeded to make a set of derogatory comments about Cambodian people.

At my boyfriend's family dinner, the sons were talking about the Hmong people of Cambodia and making derogatory comments stereotyping that they were stupid because they ate dog. Suddenly they looked at me and said, "Oh my gosh, T, I'm sorry. You're not Cambodian, are you?" I was shocked. When they were making these comments, I felt very uncomfortable, but I did not say anything. Instead, I just sat there like a passive victim. However, when they realized their blunder, I walked out. It never occurred to me that they were ignoring me because of their White privilege. My boyfriend, who walked out with me asked me why I didn't say anything. I just told him to forget it, that it didn't matter, and that it wasn't going to make much of a difference. Now I wish that I had spoken up. I wish I had told them how hurt and angry I was that they stereotyped Asians that way and that they had the gall to say things like that around me. (Vietnamese American, female)

As this example brings to light, no matter how hurt and angry you are, it's very hard to confront dominants when they are busy labeling and grouping your ethnicity into one category.

In the following example, a White student is subjected to her university professor's comments. While the professor believes that his jokes are in good fun, the student is aggravated and furious at this racist humor. She deeply regrets that she was unable to speak her mind.

Last year in my intro American Government Political Science class, I had a professor who was very racist (although he probably would not consider himself racist). He made several comments in front of the class of 350 students, of which maybe 5 were African American. One example sticks out in my mind. He was lecturing on the Constitution, talking about the amendments, and said to the class in a joking tone of voice, "So, for any of you out there that want to own slaves still, I'm sorry but you can't." The professor obviously thought that he was being very witty, but I was furious. I honestly, very naively, could not believe that a professor said something so racist in front of the class. I didn't know what to do. I did not have the courage to raise my hand and say something in front of such a large group. I thought about saying something to the professor after class, but didn't. The fact that he was a professor and I was his student intimidated me. In short, I did nothing except get angry and talk to my friends about it. I don't think I will ever forgive myself for not saying something. It really bothers me that I was unable to speak my mind, so much so that I burst into tears when relating this story to a different professor of mine a few weeks ago. (White, female)

# IV. YOU'RE THE SAME—I CAN ASK YOU ANYTHING I WANT

One does not have to make a racist joke or call someone by a racist name to engage in stereotyping. Dominants often believe that one member of the subordinate group can speak for every member of the group. Again, they are using the paintbrush to lump subordinates together. Not surprisingly, then, subordinates often experience being singled out and asked to speak for their entire race. The assumption that there is no variability within a racial community is, of course, very ignorant. There is a whole host of questions asked to people of color that would never be asked to Whites. These questions might be considered valid and legitimate, if there were an established relationship between the discussants. However, dominants feel that their curiosity gives them the right to inquire of subordinates about anything, even when there is no established relationship. We have collected a set of intrusive questions from student journals that reflect the insensitivity of the speaker.

Are you here because of affirmative action?
Don't you love sushi? Or collard greens?

Don't you love tacos with those beans?
Doesn't Colin Powell prove that you've arrived?
Why are you people all so smart?
How did you learn to eat with chopsticks?
How do you wash your hair?
Please tell us about the African American experience.
Are all Arabs Muslims?
How do you feel about your people killing Christ?
Why must you bring the ghetto with you?
Who wears the pants in your relationship?
You don't act like you're Mexican, are you?
Aren't Jews a race?
Wasn't it horrible to grow up without Christmas?
You can probably tell me everything about China, can't you?
Do you people really eat dog?
Oh, you're getting married! Are you pregnant?
Why doesn't your dad wear a turban?
One of the questions that was almost impossible to believe was the
    following:
When you nurse your baby, does your milk come out chocolate?

Everyday actions, such as filling out a bubble-form that asks one's race
or ethnicity, points out to many subordinates that dominants assume they
are all the same. These forms force subordinates into categories that often
don't match their racial identity. In the following quote, a White woman
relates a quandary that a Persian classmate shared with her.

> The girl I was sitting next to in class today explained that she was Persian.
> She said that it was very difficult for her because she did not know where
> she fit in—was she White? Was she Black? Her entire culture/ethnicity has
> been overlooked by American society, so she has to check "other." How
> would I feel if I had to check "other"? I don't think I would take it as well
> as she did. (White, female)

As this example shows, dominants (who of course make the forms) expect people to conform to their definitions of racial and ethnic groups. By
forcing subordinates to fit into the categories that dominants provide, subordinates are forced to ignore their entire culture and identity.

As stated at the outset of this section, people of color often find themselves being called upon to act as the "spokesperson" for their race. They
are asked to speak for all African Americans, or all Asians, or all Latinos, a
task which, of course, is impossible. This task is particularly daunting for
people who are not comfortable speaking out. In the following excerpt, a

biracial female relates a story of a shy young man who was constantly called upon to give the "Black perspective" in his sociology class at UCLA.

> There were about 30 students in the class but T was the only African American. In this class, our professor tended to always call on T, singling him out, but I don't think that he was even aware that he was doing it. T is a quiet guy and was never really one to participate in class discussions but it seemed like, in this class, he had no choice. For example, we would watch some sociological movie on a troubled kid (who happened to be African American). After the movie, during discussion, the professor would specifically ask T what he thought about the movie or other questions about what he thought the kid was feeling or thinking at specific parts of the movie. When this happened, I could easily see the discomfort in T's face. After class, he would tell me how much it bothered him because he felt like he was being singled out because he was the only Black guy in the class.[1] Just because he was Black and so was the main character of the movie, this did not mean that they have some kind of connection or that T would experience the same feelings as this kid in similar situations. T did not want to be a spokesperson for his entire race . . . he was not an expert. He also felt that when we talked about racism in our class or anything else that had to do with African Americans, that people in class tended to look at him. (Biracial, Japanese White, female)

Subordinates are not only asked for the perspective of their entire group, but they are often challenged with everything that dominants find puzzling or irksome about their race. They are, for instance, asked to justify Black politics, or explain how people can possibly eat a popular food in their culture. In the next example, an African American woman reviews her own experience with being bombarded with intrusive and racist questions from her White peers in high school.

> Because I was one of the three Black people in my high school (the other two being my sisters) I was, for many people, their only encounter with a Black person. I was the standard of Black that all of my friends and acquaintances thought Black people should try to achieve. Every time there was a racial issue that was burning the covers of newspapers and magazines, I would have to be the voice of all Black people, everywhere. They would ask me, "Why are Black people still so stuck on slavery? That was 400 years ago." So as not to rock the boat, my reply would always be, "Some people just can't stop living in the past." I would always try to give an acceptable answer. Not the answer that would make me look like an activist or something. They always thought they were paying me a compliment by saying I wasn't like the other Blacks, I was different. The White

---

[1]This professor's cognitive assimilation means that the person that falls within a category is seen as more alike than they may actually be. See Sampson, 1999.

people loved me. I was always "that cool Black girl." I was extraordinary, because my parents had money and I didn't speak "that ghetto shit." It was okay for the most racist people to be friends with me because I wasn't like the other jungle bunnies. I was different because I wasn't a threat. I didn't remind them of the millions of people that are still stuck in hell because of racism and slavery. I don't remind them that they are where they are today because they stand on the bones of migrant workers, slaves, and even poor White people. I was never really comfortable in my own skin because I believed that someone else's skin was more special than mine. I no longer believe that. I love the person that I am, skin color, hair, lips, and all. (African American, female)

Many of the questions posed from peers to college students of color derive from stereotypes. In the following example, a White male talks about how he and his wife, a woman of color, are hounded by questions. The questions his wife has been asked are astounding for their ignorance, their intrusiveness, and the way the speaker turns the subordinate into an object. She no longer is identified as a student, a daughter, or a wife. Rather, she is continually pigeonholed by the stereotype of a Japanese woman.

My wife of 7 years is Japanese. Some of the things said to and about her have ranged from ignorant to downright stupid. On campus, a person asked her if she was mail order bride. Another asked her if she eats dogs. If these people were being mean, at least I could understand it, but in most cases these people are being honest. The most common response I get from men when I tell them that my wife is Japanese is a knowing nod, followed by "she does everything for you doesn't she?" (White, male)

# V. YOU'RE THE SAME—YOU HAVE NO FUTURE

The most common, demeaning image, and perhaps most consequential stroke the paintbrush delivers, indicates to subordinates that they are not destined for success. They are painted as less intelligent, less motivated, and generally less capable. Even when subordinates prove these stereotypes wrong, dominants try to paint over their abilities. Because dominants are typically in positions of power their paint job often works.

Moreover, in their efforts to preserve self-interest, dominants promote their own beliefs about who shall be successful. The brush is used to paint "F" for failure on subordinates' talents, abilities, and hopes. There is no need to paint a white "S" for success; success is synonymous with Whiteness. The brush must work to ensure and justify how failure and denied opportunities are designated for some, whereas security and prosperity are designated for others. The painters teach subordinates their proper place in the collective; a collective in which subordinates of varying racial backgrounds are generically categorized as being the same.

In the following excerpt, a young man learns about his value and his occupational future from his sixth-grade teacher. She makes it clear that success is not in his future because he is African American.

> I know now the teacher was probably racist and had no care in the world about my feelings when she also told me it would be hard for me to become successful because I looked Black. (African American, male)

In our second example of blatant racism, an African American student discusses the painful and damaging message that his teacher explicitly provided for him when she equated his Blackness with failure, stupidity, and an inability to achieve his dreams.

> School and home were two very different places for me. At school, I learned all about racism and becoming prejudiced. The town nicknamed "Klancaster" (known to outsiders as Lancaster) possessed some very racist teachers in the classroom. In the sixth grade, a teacher said to me that I would never become a lawyer because I was Black. (African American, male)

For many dominants, it's a given that teachers will be kind and supportive and will push them to achieve their full potential. However, for this young man, and others like him, teachers and other adults placed obstacles in their path of progress and success.

Teachers and counselors can also do damage even when they feel they are being kind and understanding. In the next example, a Latina student describes her experience with being racially stereotyped by her college counselor. This counselor who would resolutely deny that she is racist seeks to paint all Latinas as similar. Specifically, her expectations of Latinas are that they should not be pre-med majors.

> When it entered my mind that a professor could be using racism to give me a lower grade, I thought that I should be ashamed of myself for thinking in such a way. Therefore, I pushed the idea out of my mind and accepted my grade because I had not studied enough. It wasn't until I wanted to drop the class one quarter because I was having family problems and could not handle 12 units. I made an appointment with a counselor, who was a big White lady in her sixties. When she asked me why I wanted to drop the class, I confided in her and told her about my problems at home and how it was too stressful. I could not believe what she said. She said that it was typical of students like me to go through such problems at home and that I shouldn't worry. "Students like me!" What did she mean by that? This made me so angry but what made me even angrier was when she saw the notation on my folder that I was pre-med. She tried to convince me that with the problems I had, I probably would not be able to handle pre-med,

and that I should consider going into another career. I was pissed but I calmly told her that I was sure that these kind of problems would not be there forever. "Trust me," she said . . . I know that she was referring to Latinos in general. She was stereotyping me as coming from a broken family full of problems that just never go away. She also inferred that because I was Latina, I was a high risk of dropping out. I was so mad. I thought that this type of discrimination from a UCLA staffperson could not happen to me. (Latina, female)

Students of color recall, with great vividness, incidents in which others degraded their intelligence and opportunities. The internalized pain and rage is enduring. In the next example, an African American male talks about his fifth-grade experience with racism. He learns that success and good grades were only for White students. The lesson is made very clear: Only White students succeed and have good grades.

When I received my report card it was usually safe to assume that I received straight A's. There was no reason for me not to get straight A's. I excelled to the top of my class in every subject. To my surprise I glanced at my report card and Miss W had given me a B. She did not give me a B+, she gave me a B in spelling. I was very disappointed. She suggested that I talk to my mother about my grade and possibly have a conference with her.

When we arrived at the school my mother asked Miss W why I had received a B instead of an A. When Miss W showed her my test they had mostly received grades in the high 90s. When my mother questioned why I received a B with such high test scores, Miss W said it was because I missed some homework assignments.

When my mother asked which homework assignments I missed she said she had those records at home and my mother would have to take off work again to schedule another meeting to see them. My mother knew that I had turned in all my work. She had already talked to my math teacher who told my mother that I should have received an A and Miss W is grading me very unfairly. As my mother and I walked back to the car she talked about how Whites treat Blacks unfairly because they are prejudiced and don't like to see Black children excelling past White children in the classroom. (African American, male)

We often like to believe that grades are objective measures of our achievement in the classroom. As this example demonstrates, teachers have a great deal of arbitrary power. Though there is often solid evidence, such as tests and homework, that can be used to either "prove" or "disprove" a teacher's assessment, they can choose to make it hard for students and their families to have access to these materials. For instance, this student's mother was forced to take off 2 days of work to try to investigate her child's grade. The myth of "objective grades" is one of the factors that lead some people to vehemently oppose programs such as affirmative action, which try to compensate for disadvantages and discrimination that students of color experience throughout their education. However, as these excerpts show, for many students, the struggle to get good grades means more than doing assignments and studying for exams. It also means battling prejudice.

For many students of color, arrival at the university suggests that they have overcome a great deal. However, they are rarely given a warm welcome. It's as if the paint is continually reapplied to newly emerging identities. When students describe their experiences in college, they report how the paintbrush operates in their classes and in their everyday life with peers and professors. In the following excerpt, a Korean woman articulates what many dominants express when they encounter students of color on campus.

> I grew up thinking that all Mexicans were meant to work for us (Koreans). I have to admit that when I first came to college, only about 2 years ago, I did wonder how most Latino/as got here to UCLA. Affirmative action, perhaps? I mean I worked my ass off to get into this school, they probably got in by affirmative action. Then I actually had an intelligent conversation with a Latina. I was ashamed to think what I had thought. All my life my family, my community, had labeled them as inferior, as illegal immigrants. How could I change my beliefs now? I realized I had to, that I would be destroyed in my prejudice if I couldn't. (Korean, female)

This woman's experience is fairly common. The publicity over affirmative action has made all minority admissions seem suspect. Unfortunately, concern about preferential treatment starts in high school, as recognized in this next example.

> One incident I clearly remember regarding my ethnicity occurred my senior year of high school. W, a girl who hung out in my group of friends, made a comment to me about not having to worry about getting into UCLA because of my last name. When she made this comment to me I remember being very offended. Immediately I defended myself. I felt that she was wrong for making such a comment and wondered why my friend would say such a thing to me out of spite. She was also applying to UCLA and was afraid of not being admitted. That day, I recall comparing our grades, scores, and activities and once we had finished, W had nothing to say. She knew that after we had compared our applications that I had a better chance of being admitted. This incident that I have just briefly explained was the first time I had ever been bothered by my last name. I did not want the last name Chavez because I felt like it automatically screamed out "minority," please let her in. These feelings made me want to change my last name on my college applications just to prove to everyone that I could get into the school of my choice based on my academic merit and well-rounded involvement. (Bicultural, Mexican Portuguese, female)

Affirmative action is designed to help disadvantaged students based on merit. This challenges the dominants' sense of their own privilege. The anti-affirmative action sentiments made by dominants attach a stigma to it. This often causes subordinates to feel insecure and pressured that they have more to prove. These fears are often confirmed as students interact with professors, who also assume that they are not as competent or need more help than their White counterparts. In the following example, a university professor's assumptions about students of color are immediately apparent in his greeting to a Mexican Portuguese woman.

I was discriminated by a professor my freshman year at UCLA. When I went to my professor's office hours to discuss a paper assignment, he assumed I was there to talk about a midterm I had taken the week before. When I told him my name he replied with "oh, did you do bad on your midterm and want to see your exam?" Although he was nice, he assumed I had done bad on my midterm and suggested going over the areas I didn't do well on. I was offended, he heard my name and then assumed I did not do well. He made an assumption based on the stereotypes society has placed on Latinos which are something like Latinos are not intelligent, they may struggle in learning and very rarely excel rank in the top 20% of their classes. (Mexican Portuguese, female)

This professor was not as openly racist as the elementary school teachers discussed earlier in this section. But the assumption that he made, that the student must have done poorly on the exam given her race, is a stereotype that is equally damaging to the students' self-esteem.

# VI. YOU'RE THE SAME—YOU RUIN "GOOD" NEIGHBORHOODS

Americans move quite frequently. In fact, almost 20% of all Americans move at least once a year. When dominants move, they expect to be greeted with a "welcome wagon" committee knocking on their new house and helping out with small gifts and information about schools, shopping, and church. They also want information about the percentage of subordinates in the area. Moving and buying what one can afford is perceived by dominants as a basic right belonging to everyone. However, it is a right that is denied to many families of color. When people of color move into a predominantly White neighborhood, they are often treated like a plague or disease that would surely destroy property values.

I moved in with my grandmother's sister and my aunt when I was 10. I grew up in Arcadia all the way up to high school and I would overhear people say throughout the entire time, even some of my own friends and their family would say things like: "I can't believe all these Asians are storming in. These people are taking over our neighborhood." I found this so hurtful that it made me cry. Why was it their neighborhood? My family worked so hard with their blood and sweat to buy the house. Was this not America, the land of equality? This invisible racism is worse than the blatant form, for things are sugarcoated to seem like everything is equal, when in actuality they are not. I did not know it at the time, but this type of prejudice created much internalized oppression inside myself and therefore I felt this great pressure to fit in. I think this is why most of all my friends were White in elementary, junior high, and high school. (Korean, female)

Even when subordinates go out of their way to prove that they are friendly neighbors, they can still find themselves faced with prejudice. In the following excerpt, a female student already living in an apartment extends herself to her newly moved-in neighbors. After going out of her way to be helpful and informative, she asks to borrow something and is blatantly rebuffed.

Last year, a White couple moved into our building. Now, you can just imagine that when they saw me they were a little surprised. So, I was cool. I let them know that it was not safe to park in the lot, etc. etc. But, one day I wanted to borrow their vacuum, so I asked. The husband goes and gets it for me and he begins to hand it to me. Right then, the wife walks out and says, "Oh honey, don't you remember the vacuum doesn't work?" He looks at her like "what the hell are you talking about?" And then she leans forward looks him straight in the eye and raises her eyebrows and says, "Remember, it's broken." Then he says, "Oh." Right then I knew, I shouldn't even try to deal with them. My encounters with them thus far have included a nasty encounter regarding my poor parking, refusing to answer the door when I needed help, and quick stares when I am nearby. They (or she) have a problem with race, and they did not even need to tell me. I know, just by their actions. (African American, female)

Like the couple just described, many dominants stop short of being openly racist. But their transparent acts make it clear that they don't like or don't want to have anything to do with minorities. Next, another woman describes the pain associated with looking for apartments near UCLA when you are African American.

I remember one incident when we were in Palms looking for an apartment. We were trying to get the feel of the area in terms of price range, so we went to a couple of dumps, i.e., places we knew we weren't interested in, and asked about the cost of rent. We got to this one place, and went to knock on the manager's door. No one answered. We could hear noises inside. In fact, to this day I'm sure the manager looked through his peephole. Well, we heard the TV, so we kept knocking, persistently. Finally, this big, stinky, old White man with no shirt on comes to the door and very rudely says "Yeah? What's the problem?" I said, "We're inquiring about the two bedroom apartment for rent." He said, "You got a job?" I said, "Excuse me?" He said, "What do you do?" I was shocked!! So my friend asked "And how much is the rent for?" He said 1,100 dollars a month. After that we just left. I knew that place was not worth that much. In fact, it could not have been more than $650. I was so hurt! I kept voicing my astonishment to my friend. She was not even moved by the situation. It was like it didn't even phase her. I couldn't imagine how anyone could be so cruel. Even though I didn't want to stay in the dump, I felt limited. I hated that feeling. (African American, female)

For this young woman, being a student and part of the UCLA community was not enough to diminish her Blackness. Simply because of her skin color, she would not be given a choice of the full range of available apartments. Her choice is circumscribed.

# VII. YOU'RE THE SAME—YOU LOOK SUSPICIOUS, AND I CAN'T TRUST YOU

Subordinates are continually subject to inspection and suspicions. The simple sight of a subordinate will lead to an evaluation. In that process, they are all too often seen as dangerous or threatening. They are often lumped together as criminals and thieves. In the following excerpt, a student is with her father, as he is closely scrutinized. Her father playfully but painfully acknowledges this inspection when he failed to pass the border patrol's scrutiny. One can only imagine the self-degradation.

Two months ago, the border patrol stopped my dad and I in San Clemente. The officer asked if the car, which I had bought recently, was his. As my father reached for his license, the cop reached for his gun. My dad said, "I'm just getting my license." The cop responded, "Oh! You have a license?" At first I was shocked, then it was followed by outrage. I told the cop I had a license, too. The cop checked both of them and they just waved us through. We drove about a mile in silence and then my dad said, "I guess we're too brown today." (Latina, female)

Although not all inspection is life threatening, as it was in the previously described incident, fear and suspicion of people of color often leads to outright mistreatment. In this next excerpt, an African American student described her humiliation at the hands of a dominant, who never apologizes for the false accusation.

I know how it feels to be on the other side of the White privilege. When I was younger, I went into a store and the White owner served other White people that came in the store even after I was there for 10 minutes. He never asked if I needed help. He did not really acknowledge my existence. After I looked around for a while, I walked out and he followed me into the next department store. In front of everyone, he asked me to empty out my purse on the counter because he thought I stole something from the store. I was embarrassed and ashamed. I was standing there with everything I had in my purse, by myself, with everyone watching me and not one person defended me or tried to help. They just stood there as if I had done something wrong. He never apologized for embarrassing me, he just walked away without a word. (African American, female)

Here again, we can see the general power of the white paintbrush. This woman, who was a consumer and not a criminal, was subject to examination and humiliation because of her skin color. Instead, the storeowner felt so justified in his assumption that the Black girl might be stealing, he never apologized for his unfounded accusation. Thus, if his actions caused her to feel ashamed, that wasn't his problem, it was hers. It was part of her legacy as a subordinate.

# VIII. YOU'RE THE SAME—YOU'RE UNIMPORTANT SO I NEVER HAVE TO NOTICE YOU

Sometimes, the paintbrush doesn't work to make difference obvious, but rather to make people who are different feel invisible—along with their pain, their needs, and their accomplishments. We eat fruit picked by migrant laborers, whom we don't think about. We enjoy dinners without noticing the bus boy. We enter our office everyday without thinking of the janitors who made it possible for us to continue to fill our wastebaskets. Invisible subordinates often do the shit work of society: removing garbage, cleaning streets, mowing lawns, cleaning homes, and changing diapers.

Similarly, invisibility is something that often occurs to students when they shop. They are made to wait or are simply ignored. A Muslim woman describes her experience with being ignored at a make-up counter in a major department store.

I was at the make-up counter at Macy's and there were two women behind the counter talking. I knew what I wanted to buy and I was just waiting there for someone to help me. But they never even bothered to ask me if I needed any help. Just then another woman (older, White) walks up to the counter and automatically one of the girls walk up to her and asks if she needs any help. Well, I'm not the type to cause a scene, so I was so upset that I just left. I realize that maybe it wasn't my race, but maybe they thought that I didn't have the money to afford their products, whereas this older lady looked wealthy enough and old enough to afford it. (Middle Eastern, female)

Like many people of color, this woman was left to wonder—was it because of race that she wasn't helped? Or, was it because of something else? These questions, along with the accusation of "you people make everything a race issue," haunt people of color. But, the journals are clear on at least one point: Invisibility is a common experience, one that is even noticed by some dominants.

A White woman describes her experience in a yogurt shop. She sees and defends the invisibility of a Black man.

> I told the class about how this weekend I went to a yogurt shop. Four of my female friends and I had already been helped and the employees were asking the crowd of customers who was next (they help based on numbers so they were asking who had the next number). A Black man had the next number and he was telling the guy asking that he was next. The guy behind the counter blatantly ignored him and continued to ask my friends and I what we wanted. I repeatedly told him that we had already been helped and that the gentleman waiting at the counter was next. The guy kept ignoring the Black man and I cringed. I finally screamed at him, "He is next! He has the next number. We were last, and he has the number after us. Can you not see him?" I walked out, telling them that I would never eat there again. (White, female)

Here, we can see that people who work retail have the power to determine who is worth serving. The consequence of this power is to be able to make people of color constantly question themselves. "Was it race or was that person just rude?" "Did I do something wrong?" These are issues that dominants don't have to deal with. For them, bad service is just bad service. They walk away and never have to think about it again. They can give a poor tip and be finished. They rarely have to be concerned about being judged by their race.

We need to ask what happens when the person cannot be marked racially. In other words, what about those individuals whose physical appearance does not fall within the categories that have been established by dominants? Their differences and similarities cannot be readily identified and thus, oppressed by those in power. Therefore, biracial and bicultural people challenge the dynamics of the dominant-subordinate relationship. How dominants and subordinates respond and react to these individuals is the subject of the next chapter.

# STUDENT TESTIMONIALS

*Voices of Pain and Voices of Hope* opened up my eyes and heart to what other ethnicities go through from day to day. It helped me to realize that there are still prejudices going on in our society. After reading *Voices,* it encouraged me to have open dialogue with my friends from different ethnic backgrounds, as well as becoming an advocate for different ethnicities.

**Julie Kreiger, White, Female, Psychology Major, California State University, Northridge**

I have always been a strong believer that people are not born racist—they are socialized to be racist. Through Jerome Rabow's introduction of the paintbrush in *Voices of Pain and Voices of Hope,* I learned that people are painted to become racist by their families and peers. I found myself nodding in agreement while reading Rabow's work because I strongly related to many of the experiences students had with racism. Although different painters have painted us all with different brushes, I learned I have the ability to confront these racist paint strokes. This book has allowed me to look within myself to get rid of the paint strokes in my life.

**Cynthia Pineda, Guatemalan, Female, Student, University of California, Los Angeles**

Reading *Voices of Pain and Voices of Hope* opened my eyes to the reality that racism not only persists, but also thrives in this country, in this "liberal" state, in this diverse metropolis of Los Angeles, in my circle of friends, and within me. It inspired me to change the way I think and act, not only to silently acknowledge the evils of the ubiquitous racism in this alleged melting pot, but to open my mouth and speak up for change. This book has the power to make the world a better place for all of us.

**Carey Snowden, White, Female, Senior, University of California, Los Angeles, Biology Major**

*Voices of Pain and Voices of Hope* has allowed me to see the pain that everyone goes through. I feel that most of the oppression I have received has mainly come from other African American people. If my people are able to stop judging one another on such a negative level then as a group we can fight oppression together. I say *my people* because that is to whom I identify with and feel most comfortable around. Although the majority of prejudices and stereotypes had come from people within my community, this is not to say that White Americans have also not hurt me with their comments. It is deeply unfortunate that people from my own community do the dirty work of oppression without realizing how they learned these prejudicial behaviors. *Voices of Pain* helped me understand how we all function in a context of discrimination.

**Romeisha Troupe, African American, Female, Student, California State University, Northridge**

# V

## Arbitrary Strokes:
### The Multiracial Experience

*With the Assistance of*
June McIntyre and Hollyann Simonson

We have documented how the power, privilege, and insulation of dominants allow them to either pathologize subordinates as "different" or cluster subordinates as "the same." In both scenarios "the other" is less. All invariably experience these messages—messages that are biased and racist. Though the lessons on how to respond to "the other" are more ambiguous, what happens when a dominant isn't sure of a person's race? What happens when a dominant doesn't know whether they should paint, what to paint, or what color to use? What happens to the biracial person when a dominant can't categorize the "other" into his or her schema of racial categories?

This chapter will explore how dominants and subordinates treat people of mixed race and ethnicity and how multiracial persons respond. Biracial and multiracial people pose a challenge to dominants and subordinates because their membership in any particular ethnic or racial group is not clearly discernable. The add variety to the distinct racial categories upon which Americans rely.

In Section I, we show how dominants respond to multiracial persons with a set of questions. Section II shows how dominants force categories upon multiracial people. Section III describes the naming process that endures. Section IV describes how subordinates also pressure multiracial people to choose a single identity. Finally, Section V demonstrates the responses of multiracial persons to their treatment by dominants and subordinates.

In the following excerpt, we begin to discover what dominants do when their schema for racial classifications is challenged. A Japanese American female describes the constant questioning of her biracial identity. She has coped with such inquiries for most of her life. She explains how dominants categorize and evaluate. Her name is a marker that has created expectations for painters. The painters are often disappointed when they meet her in person. This woman struggles to find acceptance by dominants and continues to feel somehow inferior.

I'm ¾ Asian and ¼ White and I consider myself biracial because my experiences have largely been shaped by my mixed backgrounds. I have a White last name although I look mostly Asian. From elementary school and on, I have had to deal with people harassing me, asking for a detailed explanation as to why I have a White last name. It makes me feel almost as if something is wrong with me. Sometimes I feel like just saying that I'm adopted, just to make things easier for me. I'm 22 years old, and I would say that for a majority of my life I have had to explain myself, almost in need of justifying my existence. People are always asking me, "what's your last name?" or "why is that your last name?" When I tell them, they proceed by asking more questions concerning my racial identity. It's as if every single person of any race needs to know how Asian I really am. It's amazing how my name has really affected me. My name is a racial marker, an identifier for other people. If I didn't have a White last name, no one would even assume I was anything other than Asian. I also feel that whenever I meet people face-to-face after having mentioned my last name prior to the meeting, I am disappointing them when they realize I'm not really White. For example, there was a time I was conducting interviews I told the interviewees my name over the phone, and when I met them, their reactions made it seem like I wasn't good enough. I felt like they expected me to be White then realized upon meeting me that they DO NOT have me all figured out. Now, of course, this may be me projecting, but what are most relevant and valid about these personal experiences is that I do have to think about these things. Sometimes I think, "Should I tell people that I'm not really White, that I'm mostly Asian?" I cannot believe I'm in this position where I really think that sometimes, even though I know I shouldn't have to ever explain myself. The struggles I experience as a biracial woman is part of my everyday consciousness, because somewhere inside of me, I feel that I'm not good enough, that it's my duty to almost warn people that I'm Asian. As an employee, it's like telling prospective customers that what they think they are buying is not what they expect, that it is faulty in some way, that I am faulty in some way. (Biracial, Japanese American, female)

It is a daily fact of life for biracial students to be forced to select a racial category and explain their existence. The backdrop to these ongoing interpersonal encounters is the deeper issue of power.

Dominants are vigilant about preserving their power in society. They always ponder on whom shall be granted access and who will be denied entry into the circles. Denying entry to all people of color would turn America into a caste-like society. This goes against our ideals and values. However, treating all as equal would also be threatening to the ongoing efforts to preserve power. But there is a subtle way to preserve power. How? By granting access to only a few subordinates, dominants can preserve their power. By providing limited access, dominants can prove to themselves (and try to prove to subordinates) that they are open to providing access to all. This is consistent with the ideals of the United States as an open, just and meritocratic society. This helps dominants assert that they are "colorblind" and that race doesn't matter. This enables dominants to believe that America is a melting pot. Because access to power is available, albeit on a very skewed basis, anyone who brings up racial discrimination is agreed to be either too sensitive, acting like a victim, or playing the race card for their advantage. Thus, painters quickly point to Colin Powell and argue that: (a) racism is dead; or (b) that because Powell has made it, this proves that anyone in America can make it. The privilege of dominant thinking allows them to "blame the victim" for their own subordinate status. If Black or Brown individuals are at the bottom of the economic or educational ladders, they must be personally flawed. While monitoring who gets into the circles of power, a problem develops for dominants when subordinates are not easily classified or categorized.

A multiracial student describes her frustrations when dominants expect her to explain and justify her physical features not typically associated with being African American.

> Although we are mixed with three or four different races, my parents and I consider ourselves Black. I have light skin and curly hair, which often encourages people to ask me, "what are you?" I mostly reply African American or Black. This never seems good enough for people. I guess because some of my features are more "White," I must justify why it is I look different from other Black people. People always ask me what I am with an answer in mind and when they don't get what they expect it's almost as if they feel cheated because my answer doesn't fit their expectations. I feel that this in a sense is the dominant's power over me to be dissatisfied by my answer. (African American, female)

Individuals from mixed heritage are continuously faced with questions about their identity. The confusion arises merely from their physical appearance and multiracial students are forced to continually prove their identity because of it. Biracial people are also pushed and pulled by subordinates. In fact, when subordinates are confronted with a biracial person who cannot clearly be identified, they also resort to questioning, naming, and categorizing as a means devalue the person who does not fit into pre-conceived and stereotypical racial categories. Subordinates living in the context of American racism act in ways that are similar to dominants.

An African American woman describes the hurt she feels when others question, tease, and challenge her racial identity.

> I completely understand about stereotypes within your own group. As a very light-skinned Black woman, people always assume that I am mixed with White, or that I am Black and Latina. I am used to questions about who I am coming from other racial groups. But comments from African Americans tend to be the most hurtful. Recently, a fellow Black student told me that I wasn't really Black; he said that I was "culturally" Black, but because I am so light, I am not ethnically or racially Black. He said that I must have more White in me than anything else. I have been called names like redbone, oreo, zebra, etc.—names that were meant as a joke, but were still hurtful, especially since I am not mixed. Would I be right for calling darker-skinned Black people names like darky? (African American, female)

Dominants seek racial identifications in order to assess an individual's physical ambiguity. What dominants want to hear are answers to explain a person's physical ambiguity, not with which racial group an individual chooses to identify. In other words, dominants do not view the multiracial individual's identity as a matter of their choice. Instead their identity is linked to one specific and neat category that the dominants believe should fit.

Dominants prevent multiracial people from asserting their plural identities because they create the standards and can assert what realities are true. They can insist upon their comfortable version of a racial reality. Though dominants in America have worked to establish clear boundaries about racial categories, race is less a matter of who is White and who is non-White, but more about who may be considered White (Hacker, 1998). Racial categories are not established forever. There is a constant debate on racial categories. The 1900 census had 5 racial designations, the 1930 census had 10 designations, and the 1990 census provided 15 options for designation of race. Race is a concept created by humans that has little scientific status. American dominants had to create a systematic and legal approach to who's Black, known informally as the one-drop rule and known formally as hypodescent. The one-drop rule states that a biracial or multiracial child is categorized under whichever parent is of lower racial status (Rockquemore and Brunsma, 2002). This rule prevented the off-spring of slaves and their slave owners from inheriting property. This rule more or less seems to still apply to other mixed-race children when there is a White and non-White parent. The one-drop rule, grounded in legal and historical traditions, still operates informally to support racial discrimination. Because American dominants claim that there are only four races, being multiracial threatens those who prefer to have their views of race as fitting neatly into one of the four categories. This chapter will document the ongoing attack on the identities of multiracial persons. One can imagine that if new racial categories were created, there would be a great multiplicity of new races. In the 2000 census, there were seven racial categories. The new census would challenge racial thinking of Americans who believe and act as if the four races have scientific merit.

Over the years, dominants have created racial categories in order for them to clarify their confusion about, or towards, multiracial people. Multiracial people are then forced to respond to these oversimplified categorizations. The rigid system of classification in the United States contributes to the unique responses of multiracial individuals. The persistent questioning of the origins of an individual's physical features and background helps perpetuate the social and institutional racism of the solution and marginalization that multiracial person experience. In turn, social institutions also force multiracial people to separate the races within them and to choose one to represent themselves. These institutional "categories" that are forced upon multiracial people are created to fulfill dominants' own general feeling of power over them.

# I. I WILL PAINT YOU BY QUESTIONS

Multiracial students frequently mentioned their experiences of being questioned. Questions such as, "what are you?" often created discomfort and unease. A biracial student describes her own uneasiness when asked to identify her ethnicity.

> It wasn't until high school until I really started to feel the impact of what being "half" of something really means. It didn't really matter what I was half of. My friends didn't really care but encounters with strangers were a whole other story. Sometimes I would get a question such as "what are you?" before I would even get a "hello." The facts that these people were assessing me for a what and not a who, troubled me. I didn't know what to do about it. Sometimes I would play games with them. My answer to that infamous question would be, "I'm a girl." To me, it was amusing to see people squirm. I enjoyed their uneasiness. It was my way of dealing, of turning the tables back in their faces. The only problem was that each time this happened, it reaffirmed the fact that most people are not willing to see my value for anything more than what my skin looks like (Biracial, Chinese-White, female)

This student copes with the continual questioning of "what are you?" by not giving answers that were expected. When the multiracial person does not comfort the questioner with their expected answer, the conclusion remains.

In the following example, a multiracial student writes about the discomfort she feels when faced with such questions. She describes how she is unable to truly identify with any of her three ethnicities.

> I have always been uncomfortable and unsure about discussing the issue of race and ethnicity. I am at a point now where I am comfortable enough to want to understand and confront myself and others . . . to extend myself and recognize that, indeed, my experiences as a Japanese/Mexican/Filipino gal growing up in Southern Orange County are significant. That the prodding and condescending questions of "where were you born?" and "where are you from?" and "you're not truly a Mexican because you're only 25% and you don't speak Spanish and you're really not Filipino either!" and the constant shock expressed on the faces of many that such a strange mix could occur . . . the possibility of my existence is shocking to most people. (Multiracial, Japanese-Mexican-Filipina, female)

Multiracial individuals are continually required to provide information about their background and to justify their existence in the world. Because of dominants' reliance on defining people purely based on their physical characteristics, multiracial individuals feel that they are sometimes not accepted as legitimate members of their own ethnic or racial group.

A biracial female describes people's insistence on "figuring her out" so that they can categorize her.

> I can tell when I first meet someone that they look uncomfortable because they don't know how to classify me. "What's your ethnicity?" and they give an explanation, "I'm just curious." And with no care to match their political correctness I reply, "I'm Black and White." And I can sense that they feel relieved because they can place me in a category. Somehow, then, they feel they know where I'm coming from. I think it's ridiculous that we can't relate to someone if we don't know his or her race. (Biracial, African American-White, female)

## II. I WILL PAINT YOU BY CATEGORIZING YOU

To deal with the ambiguity that arises from multiracial appearances, dominants press bi- and multiracial persons into categories.

One student explains how she is treated as a non-Mexican person because of her White features. She is often angry because she wants to be identified as Hispanic, but instead goes unnoticed. In Mexico, she is always addressed in English, while her darker "olive" skinned siblings are spoken to in Spanish.

> I am a part of two cultures. One being the obvious White man's world and the other the hidden Hispanic cultures. For one, I am half Hispanic and I

look White. So when my family used to go to Mexico every summer I felt like an outcast. On our family vacations, I was treated very differently than both my sister and brother. I was always asked questions in English. Now mind you—my sister and brother who both have olive skin, dark hair and dark eyes—could not speak Spanish. Yet they were always greeted and spoken to in Spanish upon being greeted. This used to piss me off . . . I wanted to be treated like I was part of the Mexican culture not as if I was a White girl there to shop and get bargains. These vacations as a child made me realize that I was different (Biracial, Mexican-White, female)

Another biracial student tells of constant attempts that place her into a particular category without any regard to her own identity.

I get so angry when people tell me, "You're not really Black" or "But you're not like them." It's so amazing the people still believe that they can construct someone else's identity and then treat them accordingly. In my life I can't remember the number of times I've heard, "But you're not like them." I can't sit down with everyone and discuss my identity, nor should I be forced to. (Biracial, African American-White, female)

In the following example, a Filipino female describes how she was unaware of the unique struggles of biracial individuals to have a legitimized identity. She learns from her roommate how biracial students are always forced to choose sides.

I never really understood the dilemma that so many biracial students go through when they fill out a simple application. I know that I am Filipino and that I can identify with my culture, but my roommate who is half-German and half-Korean has to face a daily reminder that she must choose her identity. You shouldn't have to choose, but our society places such an emphasis it causes problems for the people who are biracial. It makes you have to pick, do you love your mother or your father more? You want to say that you love them the same but it really is hard to choose. You are not able to be yourself. (Filipina, female)

The personal interactions that our bi- and multiracial students have to contend with are supported by institutions that also use classification schemas that exclude them. In this first example, a biracial male struggles with the categorical system used by bureaucratic institutions. He describes his ongoing confusion over the forms he has to complete, which force him to choose one race with which to identify.

I am always confused as to what to put down for my ethnicity. All applications have basically the same choices: White, Hispanic, African American, Japanese, Chinese, etc. But what about those of us who are mixed? Since I am half Japanese and half White, what am I supposed to do—fill out half of each box? (Biracial, Japanese-White, male)

The pressure to conform to one racial category extends beyond the walls of the university campus. In the following excerpt, a biracial female student struggles with society's preoccupation with racial classifications and its unilateral vision.

> I struggle with the fact that "biracial" is not identified as a group. Society has formed a mentality in which people identify groups to be one way or another but never in between. For example, people look at me and identify me as Latino or White . . . I wasn't conceived by a mother and father so that I would have to choose between the two. I was conceived by two people that loved each other and wanted to make a child to share both of their cultures. (Biracial, Mexican Portuguese, female)

A multiracial student discusses her anger about the personal and institutional neglect regarding ethnicities in the college environment.

> It's been difficult for me, since attending [this university], to appreciate my biraciality, and in this sense, lack of a single racial identity. In an institution where so many put so much emphasis on such, it's been difficult to deal. I don't feel comfortable with ethnic/cultural identity groups. It thoroughly pisses me off that I don't see [this university] offering me a niche where I am allowed to assess both my Japanese and Jewish heritages. It's as if the student body here, and virtually everywhere else, has always imposed on me and people like myself, to find a label. What happens if the options they give do not apply, such as college applications where there was no place for me to pencil in that I was of two ethnicities. I'm so sick and tired of trying to assess that I am of two cultures and value each of them equally. (Biracial Japanese-White, female)

## III. I WILL PAINT YOU BY NAMING YOU

Because the physical appearance of multiracial individuals confuses dominants, they tend to feel a loss of control. Instead of waiting to find out about the identities of biracial individuals, or insisting upon their choosing one particular identity, dominants prematurely label multiracial people. Just as names have been used to degrade people of color, they are also used to humiliate biracial individuals. These names indicate to the multiracial person that they are something less than human.

A White male describes the experiences of his female friend and her child in a food market.

> This weekend a friend of mine witnessed some explicit racism. I just wanted to pass this story on because it has been bugging me for the past 2 days. I am still disgusted . . .
> My friend is a White female. She had a relationship for 2 years with an African American male, who became the father of her child. Susan is

now a single mother in a mostly White community with a 1-year-old daughter of mixed ethnicity. She was in a supermarket checkout line Friday when an elderly woman behind her pointed out some kids outside. The five or six kids who were playing in the parking lot were either African American or White (about half of each ethnicity), and of both genders. The elderly woman said that she "couldn't believe that those kids would play together." She expressed disgust for kids of different ethnicities simply running around together. She then said, "before you know it they will grow up and there will be zebra babies running around." Susan turned to the woman and said "I think the friendship between those children is a beautiful thing." She then exposed her baby in the cart and said "By the way, My daughter is M, not a zebra baby."

I was very proud of the way she stood up for herself. When she told me the story I could see how pissed off she was. I don't remember ever having personally experienced any such blatant expressions of racism. I was completely disgusted that this woman lived in a nearby community of mine. (White, female)

This student develops his own metaphor about what happened to his friend as she ponders the racism that affronted her. He similarly analyzes the name "zebra" inquiring into its origin as a prejudicial slur.

I was thinking of a parallel between this lady and a cockroach. They say that for every cockroach you actually see in your home, there are hundreds around that are living outside of your vision. I think this lady was kind of like the cockroach. The fact that I know one is out there provides some evidence that hundreds more are lurking around. Although in my experience racism has not overtly presented itself all the time, accounts such as these pop up in my life periodically and provide evidence to confirm that racism is alive and well.

I'm still thinking about that lady and her thoughts. Sometimes I think I am lulled into a false sense of Utopian bliss, a world in which her and her ideas do not exist. Then something comes along and gives me a reality check. Recently this class and my friend's story have given me that check. This weekend, reality made me nervous.

I wanted to add a quick question . . . has anyone ever heard the term "zebra" or "zebra baby" to describe someone of both African American and White descent? I had never heard the term and wonder if the lady was creating her own derogatory phrases. (White, male)

Two students were quick to answer his query. The first response is from a biracial male.

I think that the analogy that you gave was right on the money. Personally, I think that far too many people believe that racism is a thing of the past or isn't prevalent in today's society. Unfortunately, many people, like the old lady in your story, are also in positions of power such as teachers, bankers, police officers, judges, Congress, etc. To answer your question, yes I have heard the term "zebra" many times throughout my life. My mother is White and my father is Black. I have felt the "stares" from people when I am in public with my mother. I have also witnessed people act "differently" towards my mother once they found out that I was their son. (Biracial, African American-White, male)

I just wanted to write and say that I have heard and used the term "zebra" when referring to people of that specific "mixture" of ethnicities. It sucks to acknowledge that I used that term. My ex-boyfriend (he was ½ white and ½ Mexican) and I (½ black and ½ Philipina) would say that if we had kids they would be zebras—although that isn't really accurate. Luckily, I have learned to really think about what I said and figured out why it is that I say certain things. It is kind of like the groups that we were split into on Wed. I have referred to myself as a mutt or half-breed. So, yes, although it is wrong, I have used zebra before. (Biracial, African American-Filipina, female)

In the next excerpt, a monoracial student recognizes the unique implications of racial stereotypes for multiracial people. She reevaluates her own use of derogatory names to label multiethnic individuals because of her frustrations as a person of color. She attributes her name-calling to curiosity:

I realize that I at times would be curious of what ethnicity a person was. I sometimes called people half-breed. I never thought the comment that I was making was derogatory. I never meant it to be a statement that was demeaning, but I now know that it is. I am able to appreciate that there are people that are a mixture of everything and that I am not helping by calling some people "half-breeds." I know that I have to be sensitive to the feelings of biracial people because I am just as sensitive [when I am] identified as something other than Filipino. (Filipina, female)

As a monoracial student of color, she realizes the pain of being racially stereotyped and recognizes that the multiracial individual faces further complications as a person without a single ethnic identity. In the following example, another monoracial female admits to her use of derogatory labels targeting multiracial people and realizes it is another tool of dominance. She had never imagined that she was prejudiced against biracial individuals.

Sometimes on campus I will see people and say to myself, "oh, she must be a 'mutt' or 'half-breed.' " I have come to realize how derogatory these labels are. Saying such things is just as bad as saying Jap, nigger, butch, or wetback. I have learned that each group is given a belittling stamp, even biracial individuals. I never really thought I could be prejudiced against biracial individuals, especially with Chicanos or Latinos. (Latina, female)

We next hear from a student who was interested in the multiethnic background of her high school peer. She describes how she was unaware of the derogatory nature of labels associated with multiracial individuals.

These labels, she states, were tools to help her understand the concept of mixed ethnicities. Now, she realizes how "half-breed" is another derogatory term used to simplify or destroy the humanity in all of us.

> I distinctly recall the first time I heard the term "half-breed." This derogatory term was used in reference to a biracial student in my high school. I remember asking this individual, "What are you?" I was interested in knowing what her ethnic background was. She told me she was biracial, half Mexican, half White. I had never met anyone with dual ethnic backgrounds so I questioned, "What do you mean you're half and half?" A friend of mine attempted to explain biraciality by stating, "She's a half-breed, kind of like dogs . . . they call dogs with a combination of different breeds 'mutts' . . . those with two breeds are. . .half breeds." It was then that I adopted the term "half-breed" to refer to biracial individuals. I am ashamed to admit that I used this term out of ignorance and lack of interaction with biracial individuals. . . . As a result of my interaction and familiarity with biracial individuals, I am now aware of how derogatory the term "half-breed" is in reference to biracial individuals. (Chicana, female)

# IV. SUBORDINATES' DEMANDS FOR ONE IDENTITY

Dominants create the categories for multiracial people. Then they patrol the borders of the classification schema and force multiracial persons to choose one. Most people would like to believe that close friends and family would never measure an individual's worth based on how one identifies racially. Our students' voices, however, illuminate that close peers paint each other. This following student describes the salience of race on her university campus. Her peers express anger towards her for identifying as multiethnic and not Mexican. She discovers that people on campus and even her own friends rely heavily on assessing her worth based on her ethnic background. To be accepted by at least one racial group, she must prove her allegiance by only identifying with that one group.

> During my stay at (UCLA), I have felt alone and somewhat of a "drifter" always looking for the "right road" (by that I mean what is comfortable to me as an individual), yet never stumbled upon that road. It all started my first year. Everyone asked me what my nationality was and this not only angered me but confused me. Why did it matter? Couldn't they be my friends based on my personality, beliefs, or interests? I soon found out that my ethnic background did matter as well as my physical characteristics. I was proud to be of multiethnic blood. However, my peers, mainly the Mexican/Latinos, believed that my sense of pride was inappropriate and I was subjected to their antagonism and hostility on many occasions. (Biracial, Mexican-Native American, female)

Another student describes how even her own friends do not give her the support and freedom to identify the way she pleases. Therefore, she turns to her parents for consolation.

> . . . But never once have I come across a peer or even a friend who will truly allow for me to be the Japanese, Filipino, Mexican individual who I am—comprised of all the things that I value . . . all the experiences and characteristics that make me feel proud, comfortable, and safe. I've always received this space and a great deal of support, throughout all of my changes, from my parents. So it isn't a surprise when I mention that I've frequently called my mother from pay phones on campus just to be assured that I can face everyone (Multiracial, Japanese-Filipina-Mexican, female)

A biracial student describes the profound effect his father had in contributing to his identity crisis. At a young age, his father shows remorse towards his son's Mexican heritage. Only later does this student challenge his father in order to assert his own identity.

> Being half Mexican and Iranian, I feel that I have the best of both worlds. At times I feel like I am caught in between. Being biracial opens new doors of opportunities, but since my father [who is Iranian] never taught me about my Persian culture, I never had a strong connection with my Persian roots. To make matters worse, I never had a strong connection with my mother's Mexican heritage because my father would always put her down and say negative things about Mexicans. These negative reinforcements by my father to my mother made me very confused when I was a child. If he put down my mother for being Mexican, then I must be a half bad person because I am half Mexican. Only later on as a teenager did I go against my father to stand up for my mother and for myself, and I am proud of my mother and myself. (Biracial, Persian-Mexican, male)

Multiracial people realize that their oppression is not only from Whites, but from people who also share part of the same ethnicity. Here, a student describes the hurt and betrayal she feels when she realizes that people of her "own kind" prevent her from asserting her identity.

> I think the thing that is most frustrating is constantly having to legitimize and validate my experiences to all people, including those who are of the same ethnicity. It always seems that others see me for their own ease and benefit. In doing so, they disregard my experiences and reality altogether. Whereas I used to believe that a greater understanding would result from other ethnic minorities, I am now beginning to feel as though I am subtly being displaced by members of my own ethnicity, not solely by Whites. It hurts so much that I'm not Japanese, Mexican, nor Filipino enough for my own peers and that this is assessed for me. I expect this abrupt displacement from dominants, but not my "own kind." I feel even more hurt and less safe when viewed in such ways by other group members because I ex-

pect it from Whites and the differences are incredibly obvious. With other people I always hope that the solidarity exists . . . that other ethnic minorities can relate to centering their lives around and making compromises for the White majority. But I guess things have changed and solidarity is defined in pureness . . . by conditions . . . and mostly by appearance and somehow, my mindset and experiences are not valid. (Multiracial, Japanese-Filipina-Mexican, female)

This multiracial student describes her own frustrations when persons of color do not accept her into their community. It seems that monoracial people of color also expect multiracial individuals to legitimize their identity. The student describes her experiences as a person of mixed ethnicity, and how her "own kind" have betrayed her. She is unable to feel like a legitimate member of their group. Also, she is faced with the issue of self-defense and subordinate mobilization for self-protection.

A monoracial student confirms the feeling of being rejected by members of her own ethnicity. This female realizes her own apparent contradiction as she describes her anger towards those who deny their culture.

Generally speaking, I would not care whether or not [a person] were biracial, but in the back of my mind I would say something like "oh, that person is so White." When it comes to my own ethnic group, and their identities, I feel strongly about certain things. I hate when people deny their own culture. By rejecting their culture, I am referring to acting too White. I am writing this right now and am seeing how I am contradicting myself. (Latina, female)

These students illustrate how multiracial people are painted by Whites as well as by monoracial people of color. They experience a "squeeze" of oppression *as* people of color and *by* people of color. Minorities who have internalized the vehicle of oppression in turn apply rigid rules of belonging or establishing "legitimate" membership. (Root, 1996) Therefore, monoracial people often shun the multiracial individual.

Similarly, another multiracial student describes how her friends use derogatory names to her. Her friends use jokes to call her names, and tease her about depicting the legitimacy of her ethnicity; they play a game of exclusion and inclusion. She is teased because of her mixed race, and stripped of her Spanish culture because she does not meet their racial standards.

I was coined as "White-washed" or "coconut" (Brown on the outside, White in the middle). When they would make fun of me it was always in the form of a joke (they would all laugh afterwards, including me), or they would speak Spanish at times and then a few minutes into the conversation someone would look at me and say, "Oh! You don't speak Spanish, do you?" This would infuriate me more (although I wouldn't let them see) than the name-calling because my Mom's and Dad's entire family speaks Spanish. I feel like I have been robbed of my Spanish culture and have to endure the pressure from my peers. (Multiracial, Spanish-Native American-Irish, female)

# V. BI- AND MULTIRACIAL STUDENTS RESPOND
## A. Passing

So far, we have illustrated how the need to classify and evaluate the multiracial individual is based on the emphasis on a physical appearance that is not easily categorized, and how frustrating and painful this can be. A multiracial person can also respond to the dominants' heavy reliance on physical characteristics by turning the tables on the dominant via "passing." Bradshaw (1992) explains:

> Passing is the word used to describe an attempt to achieve acceptability by claiming membership in some desired group while denying other racial elements in oneself thought to be undesirable. The concept of passing uses the imagery of camouflage, of concealing true identity or group membership and gaining false access.

Bradshaw notes that the phenomenon of passing is associated with marginality, in which particular racial groups are stigmatized. Passing is one way multiracial people respond to their stigmatized role as a result of their physical ambiguity. Thus, the multicultural individual is aware of racial privilege in certain contexts as he or she "passes" to feel more comfortable.

Some individuals describe their ability to "pass" as a benefit because it allows them to identify differently in various situations. Others see the ability to "pass" as a double-edge sword because often individuals who chose to pass find themselves shunned by their own racial groups. A student of mixed race describes herself as a "chameleon" (Kich, 1992) whose racial ambiguity allows her to temporarily benefit from White privilege in certain situations. This woman who is White, Asian, and Native American can "pass" as Mexican among her friends. Thus, she can benefit from White privilege while not wanting to be White (which she is), and wanting to be Mexican (which she is not).

> When I think about it though, I realize that in some ways I benefit from being able to pass as White. I think that my ability to "pass" depends a lot on the people I am with. When I was in high school, most of my friends were Mexican, so when we would go out I would always be assumed to be Mexican and in this situation it was beneficial for me to be perceived this way.

My friends even gave me the nickname Jenita, so that my name would sound Mexican. I would even do my bangs high so that I would fit in better with my friends. My friends were by no means "cholas." I think that in this period of my life, I actually wished that I was Mexican. I did not feel like I fit in with the White people at my high school. At the same time I also think that I benefited by being racially ambiguous. I felt almost like a racial chameleon. Like I could pass for almost anything just depending on the ethnic make-up of the group I was with. (Multicultural, White-Sioux-Korean, female)

Another biracial student describes her ability to gain access to White privilege as she "passes" because of her "ambiguous looks."

. . . I have come to realize just how prevalent white privilege is in our society, and how, though I'm half Thai and half Eastern European, my neutral/ambiguous looks allow me to profit from those White privileges. I can catch a cab the first time I try to hail one, unlike some African Americans, and I can receive prompt and cordial service unlike some Latina women. Such simple, everyday "conveniences" are granted to me through White privilege. . . . Being denied service, being watched while shopping, or being ignored at a restaurant have never been my realities, and I know that most of it is due to my mixed looks that nobody can place. (Biracial, Thai-Eastern European, female)

This student describes the very source of the dominant's frustrations because ambiguous physical features make it difficult to know whom to oppress. The student realizes that she "benefits" from her racial ambiguity because the painters identify her as a "normal" White house instead of a house with irregular and "abnormal" hues. Kich (1992, p. 312) describes this as the "chameleon ability" which fosters temporary privilege and a sense of freedom and relief from the restrictions of being "both" and "neither." This chameleon ability makes occasional "passing" possible for the multiracial individual but is confusing for some dominants that insist on distinct racial categories. It is difficult for multiracial people to please any one group because White dominants and monoracial people of color are painters who prevent multiracial people from asserting their own identities.

The next student who details the complexities of his multiracial experiences illustrates this difficulty of acceptance. The Mexican community disregards his Hispanic identity and the White community categorizes him as Mexican because of his physical appearance.

It has been very difficult for me to understand my race and my place, ethnically. Although I am half White, have grown up in a White town, gone to White schools, and prayed in a White church, I am automatically seen as a Mexican by all people who don't know me because of my physical features. Because of this, and my anger towards the prejudices, which I have seen in my hometown by Whites, I have claimed and will claim Mexican American as my ethnicity. Naturally, because part of me is being discriminated against, I will protectively side with that half. My problem (if it is one) is my inability to relate with "real" Hispanics. The White community sees me as Mexican because of my physical appearance, yet the Mexican community sees me as White because of my White upbringing. Because I have been raised in a White society I feel deprived of my Mexican background. (Biracial, Mexican American, male)

While emphasis on having to prove one's ethnic legitimacy for the comfort of the dominant group can lead to "passing," this is not without some important consequences. In the following excerpt, a biracial and multicultural student describes how justifying her ethnic legitimacy has plagued her and caused her to feel distanced from both races.

I have always felt a void in my life when it comes to racial issues because I could never truly identify with one party, and hence, felt my "allegiance" and cultural pride lacked for both ethnicities. Though I've been told my features tend to look more "White" and I have, consequently, reaped the benefits of White privilege, I can also identify with issues involving Asian Americans. Yet, because of this dichotomy, I seem to have been disregarded and gone unrecognized by both groups. (Biracial, Japanese-White, female)

The student's testimonies illustrate how painters, both White and non-White, prevent multiracial people from asserting their identities.

## B. Other Choices

The challenge for people of mixed race and ethnicity is to differentiate between the pictures that painters paint for them and who they believe themselves to be. These students' voices portray some of the unique struggles that face multiracial individuals. They have already recognized for themselves, that they are different from others. Facing one's struggles, challenges, and the reality of the multiethnic experience lays the foundation for exploring one's ethnic identity development.

Racial categorizing, questioning, naming, and insisting upon choosing, are the responses that bi- and multiracial persons deal with. As a challenge to racial oppression, people of mixed race and ethnicity can choose, for themselves, to embrace any and all parts of their ethnic background. Some of our students are beginning to recognize that one has the right to identify the way he or she desires rather than conforming to dominant ideas of how one should be. Spickard (1992) states, ". . . these days people of mixed parentage are often choosing for themselves something other than a single racial identity."

Here, a multiracial student asserts her own identity as she realizes that the pressure to choose only one identity reinforces the power exerted from the dominant perspective. This student illustrates the way she wants to be treated rather than submitting to fixed racial categories.

When you are multiracial in this country, a choice of race is preferred so that now everyone can stop trying to figure out what you are and have you nicely labeled. But having to choose creates a dilemma, because no one side fully embraces your identity. . . . One of the most important things I have learned is that my struggle to choose was not a struggle I entered in of my free will. It's a struggle that society has wanted to place me in. Instead of running all over the ethnic spectrum, I have at this point decided to sit smack dab in the middle and define myself as mixed/multiracial. If anyone still wants to ask what I am, they better be prepared for the list. Because the truth about my identity is that I am a mix of a variety of rich and full cultures that have all been part of the traditions and values that have given fullness to my life and the lives of my family. And this mixture has occurred within the realm of American culture, which has further shaped me. Therefore, I cannot check any one box these days. So, I mark "other" and when the surveyor tries to figure out what to do with that answer, they can struggle for a solution, for it is becoming less and less my problem. I am finally entering a stage of embracing my identity, though I still face issues concerning race on an everyday basis. I am realizing that I am a taste of the future of this country. As we come closer and closer together and as intermarriages increase, as well as mixed children marrying other mixed children, the nice little boxes suddenly won't apply. Embracing the difference will become the only choice we have left. It's either that or living in self-denial. (Multiracial, Italian-Cuban, female)

This student embraces her multiracial identity as she realizes that being multiracial is legitimate, in and of itself. Another student who is of mixed race chooses to identify herself as African American. She maintains that she can assert her own ethnic identity despite the dissatisfaction of dominants.

The dominant is normally the group that actually has the problem with multiracial or multicultural people but that problem in turn makes their inability to understand who I am, my problem. I feel that my situation is unique because I wouldn't consider myself bi- or multiracial. I would consider myself African American, and when I fill out a survey I check the African American/Black box, but I feel as if I've had the experience of a bi- or multiracial person based solely on my appearance. (African American, female)

This student explores her own ethnic identity and contends that the dominants' discomfort with people of mixed ethnic and racial backgrounds is the source of her struggle. She understands that racial identification is her choice, and that it should not be about pleasing dominants. The need to question one's origins, categorize one's racial identity, and use derogatory names to label multiracial people are examples of the painters' tools of dominance. Spickard (1989) states:

> As long as "outsiders" presume to label and define the experience of biracial individuals, and as long as biracial people fail to speak out and advocate for determining self-identification, externally imposed marginality will continue. Prerequisite to embracing the right to self determination is an understanding of race as a social and political construct, primarily a tool of dominance.

Multiethnic individuals must use their voice to struggle for recognition and acceptance for ethnic legitimacy.

## VI. THE IDEALS AND NEW BILL OF RIGHTS

The bi- and multiracial students you have heard from are struggling to recover and assert lost identities. The following excerpt illustrates the struggle to deal with the other and the self.

> I was raised White and no one told me the consequences of being a minority. My mom had White privilege so she didn't know the importance of acknowledging race and what it means. As I uncovered my prejudices, I realized the fear and misunderstanding of the other (and my unknown self) was really a fear of not knowing or wanting to accept who I was seen as to the rest of the world. (Biracial, African American-White, female)

Another student has come to understand that her parent's instructions were not in her best interest.

> All throughout my life my dad has always told me that I should identify with being only White and not to worry about the other part of me because my Whiteness and the fact that I look White would take me the farthest and give me the best advantages. I now see he was wrong and that it was harmful. (Biracial, Native American-White, female)

The ongoing difficult but similar struggles of bi- and multiracial persons has led Maria Root (1996) to create a Bill of Rights for bi- and multiracial individuals. This Bill has a set of truths, which are not as yet self-evident.

**Bill of Rights:**

1. I have the right
   a. Not to justify my existence in this world
   b. Not to keep the races separate within me

    c. Not to be responsible for people's discomfort with my physical ambiguity

    d. Not to justify my ethnic legitimacy

2. I have the right

    a. To identify myself differently than strangers might expect me to identify

    b. To identify myself differently than how my parents identify me

    c. To identify myself differently than my brothers and sisters

    d. To identify myself differently in different situations

3. I have the right

    a. To create a vocabulary to communicate about being multicultural

    b. To change my identity over my lifetime—and more than once

    c. To have loyalties and identify with more than one group of people

    d. To freely choose whom I befriend and love

The voices from these student journals indicate that biracial and multiracial individuals cannot escape from the continuous scrutiny and attacks upon their identities. Painters insist and demand that the multiracial person in the United States adopt the dominant's own perceived reality; a reality that is in stark contrast to the actual identities of bi- and multiracial people.

## STUDENT TESTIMONIALS

Reading *Voices of Pain and Voices of Hope* has allowed me to reflect upon the significance of painting in the United States. As a biracial male, I recall my own encounters and struggles with coming to terms with my multiple ethnic identities. Having grown up in a single-parent household with my Japanese mother, I did not have many opportunities to learn about my Nicaraguan identity. As a result, I made it a point to discover my lost Nicaraguan identity in college. However, there were a number of concerns that I had in joining Latino student organizations on campus. I did not speak Spanish nor did I know my Nicaraguan culture. I was not sure if I looked "Latino enough" and my name did not help either. Fortunately, I became much more comfortable with my unique upbringing and began questioning societal definitions of ethnic identity. Why did I have to fear rejection from the Latino community? What did speaking Spanish, looking Latino, and having a Latino last name have to do with being Latino? I then realized that my fears stemmed from society's painted definitions of what a Latino is supposed to look and act like. Today I am constantly challenging the paintings of racial and ethnic identities in the United

States. Through my experience and that of others, I am also calling forth a redefinition of race and ethnic identities. Lastly, I am calling forth the desire for acceptance and belonging as human beings.

**Michael Miyawaki, Biracial, Japanese/Nicaraguan, Male, B.A., University of Pennsylvania, Master's Program in Sociology, California State University, Northridge**

*Voices of Pain and Voices of Hope* has not only touched my heart but shook my soul. It forced me to acknowledge the ways in which racism not only exists today but also manifests itself through those who we love (parents, family, friends, teachers). It opened my eyes to the intolerance alive today, through voices I once did not want to hear. The voices are ones that I can relate to, understand, and feel because they are voices similar to my own. *Voices* screams at me to pay attention to societies issues, as a man, a biracial, a heterosexual, a student, and an individual, and inspires me to take a stand.

**Erneal Ong, Biracial, Filipino/Chinese, Male, B.A. Psychology, California State University, Northridge**

# VI

# *Getting Rid of the Paintbrush*

What we have discovered from UCLA students is that racism was and is a daily recurring fact of life. You have heard them express their feelings and describe their experiences with race and racism, privilege and oppression. Students of color have documented the multitudinous ways they are dishonored by Whites. Minorities are also denigrated by those of their own background, as well as other subordinates. This double lack of respect is the legacy given to children of color when they are born and raised in this country. You have heard student voices describing prejudicial and racist treatment in classrooms, playgrounds, retail stores, and public spaces by parents, peers, friends, teachers, police, retail clerks, strangers, and university professors. The students' voices make plain that racism is part of the daily round of life for non-Whites. But is it enough to know and understand the ways in which children of color are treated as less? Is it enough to know that children of color are treated as similar? Is it enough to know that statements like "I don't see color" and "you're being too sensitive" invalidate the other's human experiences? Is it enough to know that the legacy of racism leads to self-oppression and self-hatred, which is difficult to change? Is it enough to know that biracial individuals are pushed and pulled to the point where they have to be chameleon-like to get along and fit in while they live with an ongoing denial of the self? Is it enough to know that the questioning of "others" as if they are "alien," "foreign," and "strange" is also part of the legacy of racism? Is it enough to know that when Whites use the idea that "because all people of color have prejudices and are therefore like us," they are refraining from examining their own racist ideology and practices? Is it enough to know that all of these questions, comments, and arguments reside in a deeper belief of the racial inferiority of people of color? In his Pulitzer Prize work, *Guns, Germs, and Steel* (1999), Jared Diamond addresses the causes of domination and racism. He feels compelled to address the biological explanation; there is no sound evidence for the existence of human racial differences

**103**

in intelligence (Diamond, 1999). Though many segments of Western society repudiate racism "many Westerners continue to accept a racist explanation privately or subconsciously."

In this text, we have not emphasized the institutional discrimination that occurs in housing, schooling, renting, loan lending, and public accommodations, which are the backdrop to daily interactions of our students. The cost of all of this discrimination is enormous. There is the lost talent of the disaffected; there are the hordes of individuals who are angry and bitter; and there are masses of people who self-segregate out of fear. There is disillusionment with our institutions of law, education, the police, and the belief in America as a democracy.

In order to move from racial oppression to race relations, groups must confront truths revealed in open dialogue; the kind of dialogue the students had with each other in class and with themselves. The students you have heard from confronted racial oppression in a forthright and honest manner. They did not reside in the comfort of their anger and denial, or the safety of their hurt and guilt. They were "ordinary people doing extraordinary things out of simple decency."[1] They did this heroically. Their decency is reflected in their willingness to listen, to acknowledge, and to accept their fellow classmates' reality and experiences. That is perhaps enough for some. But others will want more. For example, did all this talk mean anything? Did the students get beyond "feeling good"? Did the students get beyond "I now understand"? Can painters who have been so well trained and so accustomed to painting be expected to change? How long does it take to change attitude or behavior? And if changes occurred within the classroom, can we expect them to continue after students leave? Was this experience different for students of color and White students?

This last chapter documents the ways in which students were transformed by their experiences. Again the student journals will be the voices you will hear as they reflect on class discussion. The journeys taken by students of color and White students were different but we have tried to interweave the paths that each group followed. We have undoubtedly underreported paths that ended after a few steps forward. We cannot assert that all students were transformed. Not all were ready to work against racist jokes, prejudicial statements of belief, or racist actions. Indeed, a few students were not able to move forward. In the following, a Korean woman describes why she is stuck. She is unable to go beyond her years of pain, anguish, and hiding. She is not in denial about racist reality, but she feels unable to change.

---

[1]Camus cited in Judt, 1994, "The Lost World of Albert Camus," *New York Review of Books,* VXL VIII, No. 9.

I used to wish so many times that I was back in Korea when I never had to think about myself in a category as an Asian. I was just me, you know. I was free to explore and define myself with the offers that my surroundings gave me. I want to be free. I'm all tangled up inside right now. I know I can't redo time and go back to when I was in Korea, but it's too hard to deal with the past. I can't let go. Everyday, everything I do and say is reminiscent of people hurting me, treating me a certain way, seeing me in a boxed way, and I have become that. I didn't know how to fight back. I just let them define who I was and in the process I have become that. Now there is a hidden part of me that longs to come out and just be but there are too many fears and too many years of habit to cover me up and it's easier to act as if nothing hurts. Yet inside, I don't like myself for being that way. (Korean American, female)

For many, self-hatred becomes internalized. They go through life believing that they are supposed to think poorly of themselves and that everyone else views them negatively. The previous quote also illustrates the double journey the student made. One journey was about accepting self and the other about accepting others.

We certainly do not know the degree to which students were able to apply their new learning and understanding of racism into their daily lives, but many did and are still doing it. One study we completed on this class suggests that significant movements in identity occurred by the end. However, that quantitative study did not capture the struggles and issues that student's confronted.[2] Let us now examine some of the shifts that students made. The work on identity shifts in racial attitudes and behavior by Helms (1990) and Jackson (1974) documents the way in which the self is implicated with the beliefs and activities of individuals towards racism. We wish to simplify these shifts into a number of dimensions where the class aimed to achieve a movement towards a nonracist or positive racial identity. Thus we make no claims for a particular order, nor do we argue that each dimension was a necessary step for all of our students.

# I. OVERCOMING DENIAL

Denial is something all human beings do when reality becomes too painful. It is a defense mechanism that humans employ at various times in their lives. Denial comes in many forms. There can be denial of responsibility, denial of knowledge or truth, denial of actions as hurtful, and denial of the possibilities of changing racist practices. Fear seems to be a component for all forms of denial. One of the major steps taken by White students occurs when they begin to see society differently than they had prior to the class.

A White male writes about his former beliefs and his sense that the United States is a society that is open to all individuals who want to succeed. He eventually realizes the inaccuracies of his former beliefs.

> Before taking this class I honestly thought that everybody in this society, no matter what race or gender, had the same chance to do and achieve whatever they wanted in their lives if they only applied themselves. Sure, the socioeconomic background of one's family played a major role, but it could be overcome through hard work.
>
> What I did not take into account was that first of all, everything happens according to and within the White culture's rules and limitations. Secondly, even if someone from a racial or ethnic minority "makes it" in most cases there are restrictions on how far he/she will be allowed to climb up the ladder. And even if someone is compliant all the way, skin color and gender will, in the vast majority of cases, continue to set limitations no matter what one's qualifications. (White, male)

Fundamental beliefs about society are hard to modify or even change. For dominants that saw the United States as the land of opportunity and fairness, it was a difficult transition. Racism was a new reality for many of our White students. It was not obvious to them that it was alive and strong.

Until he was faced with class readings on racial identities, a 21-year-old White male had never thought about racism. Gradually he became cognizant of some of the perks he received as a White person.

> When entering this class 6 weeks ago, the idea of "racial identity" never even really entered my mind. I can now attribute that to the fact that as a White individual and a member of the dominant group, I never needed to be aware of race. My day to day actions and relationships with others has never been highly influenced by what others may think about the color of my skin. But in sitting in this class and listening to the stories and how race highly affected my fellow students (and I can now say, my friends), I realized that I have been extremely naive.
>
> I come from a middle-upper class background and have always "got what I wanted" from society in general. I have no problems with getting jobs, no problems with making friends, and no problems being understood by other people. I used to feel embarrassed if my friends and family ever saw a Mexican woman walk down the hallway and into the next door next to mine. Throughout my whole life, I have taken this kind of attitude and made them a part of who I am. I have never had reason to question them . . . until now. (White, male)

In another example, a White student describes her movement from recognition of White privilege to guilt to helplessness. She struggles with the idea that racism is her problem.

I look at my life, my experiences, and realize how privileged I've been on account of my paleness. That is when feelings of guilt turn to helplessness and frustration. I know I'm White, but there's nothing I can do about that. I can't help it that there are only peach colored band-aids at the store. It's not my fault that cops pull over minorities, and not me. It would be so easy if I could say with conviction that it's not my problem. I believe it more often than I should, and one of the things I'm trying to work on is not settling into a seat of privilege. What if I start to think that it isn't my problem, and that I can't do anything about prejudice or racism? Then I won't do anything about it. That's one of my biggest problems, and it is evident in what I've written about in my journals so far. I have a hard time recognizing that it is my problem, or rather what it is about ME that I can fix. I see it in my family, my history, my schooling, and in other people, but seeing prejudice in me is something I'm struggling with. AND IT IS SO FRUSTRATING. (White, female)

Whites are not the only students who find comfort in their denial and privilege. A Chicano female discovered her own racism and stereotypes towards Blacks. Initially, she was unable to understand her prejudices and the ways in which Latinos and Blacks have a common enemy. It was through reading Malcolm X that she became aware of her own stereotypes. While it was obvious to her that unattainable access for Latinos was the cause of poverty and lack of achievement, she had not considered this same reality for most Black communities.

I used to think that Blacks themselves created their conditions of hopelessness and poverty by being lazy, immoral, drug-addicted, and violent people. These are heavy statements to make, but racism itself is very heavy. I have never actually been in an all-Black urban community, but I envisioned it to look like the images and stereotypes I have learned from the mass media and among people I have met who painted a very racist picture. I noticed that none of these images reveals the institutional factors that have a tangible role in "keeping Blacks in their place." Because I never had a broad-based knowledge of how inequality works in perpetuating disempowerment among Blacks, I made racist assumptions on why they are always, collectively, as a group, at the bottom rung of the economic, political, and social ladder. It is because the top rungs have been removed and prevents them from climbing to higher positions.

Many of the issues that Blacks face, Latinos face as well. My own racism was confronted when I justified Latino poverty to be caused by lack of access to what Whites have and Blacks because of racist notions that they are too lazy to work. These same stereotypes can easily be turned around at Latinos too, but I refused to see it that way. Reading Malcolm X helped me see that Blacks are very determined to overcome their struggles. These barriers that we put up for them strips them of power and dignity. (Chicana, female)

Another student of color also lived in denial. Her comments are remarkable. As an African American woman, she was continually being told about racism from her family and friends, but she adamantly refused to believe them. It was only after 3 weeks of class discussions that she began to realize the painful events that she had denied.

My parents, their friends, and relatives would tell me stories of blatant, extreme racism. Yet, I wouldn't believe them. When they told me the recruiting representative at this firm was racist and didn't take African Americans as seriously as other candidates, I didn't believe them. I wouldn't believe them when they told me it was a racist act for my White friend's parents to look intrusively around our house and that because we were African American they felt obligated to check that our house was nice enough or safe enough for their child. When I heard the stories of police pulling African Americans over because they were "driving while Black" or even worse, taunting them at gunpoint, I barely believed it.

Up until a couple of years ago, I couldn't fathom these dramatic expressions of racism. I thought my parents and other such storytellers were unusually and detrimentally sensitive when it came to race. I related to many of the white students and the less conscious students in the class when they said the storyteller must be exaggerating or making a big deal out of nothing. It reminded me of myself in the past. I thought that things weren't really that bad, and I had my own experiences to prove it. I had never encountered any dramatic acts of racism.

When I started speaking up in class, the memories of the stories came back to me quickly. The ones that were too close not to be true flashed through my mind. That time when I was at a party on campus, and my Black male friend ran up to me shaking and scared. He told me that the police had just jumped him, beaten him to the ground, and accused him of some crime. I couldn't deny that that story was true. And still every dramatic act of racism aroused feelings of disbelief in me.

Remembering all the stories I have heard in my life, and suddenly remembering those things possibly blocked by a selective memory, I realize that incidents such as these have sprung up often in my life. Although they happened to friends and loved ones, they still happened to people who were just like me—and that they were true. They weren't isolated incidents, and I had formerly believed them to be, but they were a constant reality that was always manifesting itself. (African American, female)

# II. OVERCOMING SELF-HATRED

For many students of color, overcoming their self-hatred was an important step in their movement towards liberation. The students, who were targets of prejudice as children, continued to face racism as a daily aspect of their existence. As such, all have experienced difficulty with their self-worth, and all have what W. E. B. DuBois called, at the turn of the century, double-consciousness. DuBois (1906) states:

> It is a peculiar sensation. This double-consciousness. This sense of always looking at one's self through the eyes of others and measuring one's soul by the tape of a world that looks on in amused contempt and pity.

Many subordinates develop this double-consciousness at a young age. From the moment children wish their skin was lighter they begin to evaluate themselves against the dominant ideal—an ideal that destines them to fall short. And for most of these children, this double-consciousness only deepens with age. Moreover, though many of the stories related here are from years past, we should not dismiss all the infliction of pain that accompanies name-calling, body self-hatred, and lowered aspirations as merely the stuff of childhood. Though all children will undoubtedly recall one or two embarrassing and humiliating moments and experiences, the memories described by our students are multiplied over their lifetimes and the scars are enduring. Identities are established in the shadow of a White model. The self-doubt created by the white paintbrush can last a lifetime.

In the next excerpt, we see how self-contempt about one's language, parents, and physical being leads to the need to assimilate by discarding one's true heritage.

> I remember not wanting to go shopping with my mom, just because I had to translate. I didn't want others to see me as an "immigrant." I would tell my mom that I would rather go by myself. This was in high school. I would shop by myself. I was ashamed of my language. I was ashamed of my physical characteristics. I was ashamed of myself. Just like my classmates, I would use silence as a method of survival. In doing so, I wanted to blend into the mainstream society. I wanted to become someone I wasn't. I saw total assimilation as my only way of accomplishing this goal. (Latina, female)

Even as these young adults come to struggle about who they are, self-doubt still remains. Moreover, as they come to see their "inadequacies" as the results of the white paintbrush, they still hold steadfast to the idea that they are not good enough. The struggle to accept oneself as equal to Whites is difficult to overcome. In the next excerpt, a Chicano describes his feelings toward White women. He describes them as beyond his reach.

> I find women of all colors to be attractive. But I have this feeling inside of me that I am not good enough for a White girl. It's not that I think they're prettier or anything like that, it's just that I don't see them as something within reach. I maybe think they prefer to stick to their own or that I'm not good enough. I can't explain it. I believe I could approach a Latina, Asian, and Black, anything but a White. Why is that? Internalized oppression?

Maybe seeing all of these Anglos in magazines and on TV makes it seem as if they were some special untouchable. (Chicano, male)

Even when students of color have learned to value themselves, some cannot ignore the White world. They still have to live in it. In the following example, a Mexican American male discusses the difficulties involved in trying to strike a balance between loving oneself and culture and still being "American."

I feel ashamed of being Mexican American. I feel like depending on who I am with, I have to deny some part of me. When I am with White people, I feel as though I have to assimilate, and deny my Mexican heritage. On the other hand, when I am with Mexican Americans, I sometimes feel like I have to be something I'm not. Mexican Americans constantly tell me that I am White-washed, that I'm selling out, and that I'm a coconut (Brown on the outside and White on the inside). The biggest thing is that I don't speak Spanish. My father speaks Spanish, but my mother does not, and so it was never taught in my home. One individual in this class actually told me that I am not Mexican. She was not the first person to tell me that. I have no response to that, what do I say? I know I am, but she makes me feel like I'm really not, or at least she makes me question it. Either way, I feel like I can't win. If I'm with one group I feel like I have to act a certain way, and if I'm with the other I have to act another way. It leaves me with a feeling of giving up. I'm just me, and why is it not right to be who I am, listen to the music I want to listen to, and do the things I want to do? (Mexican American, female)

Overcoming the self-hatred bred by raw racism is a difficult goal for our students of color. DuBois described double-consciousness at the turn of the century. One hundred years later, our students still experience this double consciousness. It is buried deeply in the souls of children of color causing them to evaluate themselves from the perspective of the dominant.

## III. AWARENESS OF PRIVILEGE

Once we realize that someone has taught us to paint, be it our family, our peer group or society in general, a series of questions will follow. How do we put the paintbrush down? What are we afraid of? What will happen to our relationships with families and friends? Looking in the mirror at oneself is scary. We are often surprised and uncomfortable with our own reflection. This is the gift of the class, "your racism and mine." It allowed students to analyze their own identities, with an emphasis on the internalized racial and ethnic stereotypes of themselves and others. If nothing was accomplished beyond "self-awareness" of the racism that exists in all of us, then the class was a major success.

Slowly, I've been coming to see where my prejudices lie. Unfortunately, I haven't found a methodical, easy to replicate manner in which to accomplish this. It's more like accidentally bumping into a light switch in a pitch-black room, or like Wylie Coyote running off a cliff. He looks down, realizes that the ground has suddenly dropped several hundred feet below him, and he thinks, "I can't have run off a cliff, I would have seen it coming." In my case, I look down and think, "I can't have done something prejudiced; I'm not a prejudiced person." Sometimes, that eerily effective human ability to rationalize lands me back on solid ground. However, all too infrequently, I find myself falling, and recognizing some small piece of what it is that makes me prejudiced. (White, female)

In following excerpt, a student writes about the process of awareness he went though in the class. In his own words, his "blindfold" has been removed.

This class helped me become aware of the ignorance that is out there, whether it's from Whites or from other people of color. I remember the struggle between some in the class and another female student in trying to get her to recognize her privilege. I don't know if she has come to terms with it, but it seemed to me as if she was unable and unwilling to recognize it. I believe that this is the first step in getting rid of the racist attitudes and stereotypes that we have formed, and she will not be able to do this until she accepts and recognizes her privilege and uses it positively. Another example, which I remember clearly, was when another female student told the class that she didn't think racism was that big a deal and that it seemed to her that most of another female student's stories were exaggerations. This upset me because I don't imagine a person of color not being exposed to racism in their life, and in turn stating that Whites were more exposed to racism than people of color. I explained to her that she has probably been the victim of racism many times; she just didn't know it because it is too "normal" and it is so covert.

Earlier this week in class, a male student said that the people of color see all Whites as the same, and therefore he now feels like he has to show others that he is an individual, and prove that he is not like the rest of the group. I feel like this has been our (people of color) struggle since day one—trying to show Whites that we are not who they think we are, we are all different. Every day we struggle to prove to them that their stereotypes were wrong. Now it is up to Whites to show us that, and become allies.

It wasn't until I took this class for the first time that I realized that this whole time I had been living with a blindfold on. An example of this where I looked up the meaning of the word "mutt," which is what I've been referring to myself because I am multiracial. I wrote, "I knew that it meant a dog that was mixed with various breeds, but never a stupid person. Now I feel stupid for calling myself that." I am mad at myself for adopting such a negative word, and assuming that it was good, and calling myself that on a regular basis, this just shows the power of language, and how it affects everyone, whether it is positively or negatively, on a regular basis. My blindfold has finally been removed. (Biracial, Japanese-White, male)

In order to become aware of our own racist tendencies, we must also acknowledge the privilege that our race engenders. In our society, being White allows one to enjoy very specific privileges that others are not invited to behold. Specifically, White people are usually given educational advantages, job advancement, and are typically less inclined to be hassled by law enforcement. More importantly, Whites rarely face racism as a part of their daily reality and struggle. In the following example, a White female realizes that her color is like a passport or a blank check. It is always given credit and is accepted everywhere.

> I am White and I have never tried to be another color and/or race. That can be explained, though, by the fact that by being White, I don't feel the need to change. White is accepted at more places. I feel like a VISA credit card, "Accepted almost everywhere." (White, female)

Another White student acknowledges how her parents' lives and her own are much easier because of their race.

> My fellow students taught me that there are so many things that I do not have to worry about because I am White. There are places I don't even have to think about walking into. I realized how lucky I was that even though my parents were divorced and my mother supported us three kids, she didn't have to worry about losing her job because her children's skin is White. I did not have to worry about my father being killed because of the color of his skin. (White, female)

Similarly, a White female addresses her continual journey of learning about her privilege, which has led her to realize that she has not escaped the stronghold of racism. She cleverly points out the contradictory beliefs she once held. She now sees the falsehood in considering herself as a nonracist. How can you be a nonracist if you don't have any racial awareness?

> Ever since coming to UCLA, I have been on a continuing journey of learning about my "White privilege" that I have and have grown up with, and I am always discovering ways that I benefit from it in my everyday life. I grew up in a White, middle/upper class neighborhood, and really never was conscious of race issues until I got to UCLA. It was in Women's Studies 10 during my freshman year that I began to learn about people of color. This was a new term for me, although I had grown-up thinking that I was a very nonracist [sic] individual (a nonracist individual with no race consciousness . . . go figure). As my professor lectured about the ways in which women of color have been oppressed in our society, and how, in many cases, the way in which their voices have been left out of White fem-

inist discourse. I began to look at myself, and I began to realize that I too was a racist. (White, female)

A White male discusses his awareness of racism and how he can personally relate to the lessons taught in class. He begins to see that treating all people as the same is just a beginning step on a road to a nonracist identity.

I look at people of racial/ethnic minorities as well as women and gays differently now. I am acutely aware of the fact that they may come from and perceive a reality completely different from mine. That theirs is just as legitimate, and that I should be careful with my assumptions and how I, most of the time unknowingly, impose and perpetuate cultural and institutional racism while thinking that I am not racist at all. After all, my girlfriend is Black and I treat everybody in my life the same regardless of ethnicity, color, gender, or sexual orientation. This is only a tiny part of the equation, though. Actually, it doesn't mean much at all; racism has taken on a completely different, much, much further reaching meaning, and I feel rather powerless and uncomfortable about it.

Although I think that the entire process of participating in this class—the discussions, student's comments, and the readings—caused the shift in my awareness, my thinking and hopefully my future actions, I can give a few specific examples of what were real eye-openers for me:

It started with one of the student's analogy in regard to women's constant fear of sexual harassment or rape. She suggested to the men in the class to simply being locked up in a prison cell with one or more other bigger guys, who in no uncertain terms had let you know that they would, sooner or later, sexually take advantage of you. I have been arrested and briefly locked up, fortunately without such experiences, and was, for a moment, able to really feel what it may be like for a woman to walk home at night from the bus stop, down a not-so-well-lit street, and suddenly hear footsteps behind you. I will never make a comment like "What was she doing in that area at that time" or "Why was she wearing a mini-skirt" again because it ought to be completely irrelevant.

Another important contribution for me was when another student described in detail how he was humiliated and threatened to be shot during a routine traffic stop, and how afraid he was and generally how submissive he has to be, as a Black man, when having contact with the police. It brought back memories of how I have interacted with police officers in an arrogant and demanding manner, in a way that would have gotten me injured or killed had it not been for my White skin. I got away with it, though, together with some friends of mine. I even went on the offensive once, forcing a local police chief and two deputies on to a live radio talk show where we continued our attack on two particular officers for their excessive use of force. I do not regret my attitude at all, but I realize now that not everybody can act like that without putting one's self into serious danger.

The third real eye-opener came in the form of an article in our text-book, where Studs Terkel describes a 40-year-old man of Mexican de-scent's struggles with the contradictions of his understanding of himself and the American dream. He had been a "good boy" all his life, chased that American dream, and little by little come to find out that there really ex-ists no such thing for him, that the American dream means not losing for those who already are privileged. Education, opportunity, and hard work do not govern it, but power and fear. He ends up quitting corporate Amer-ica and now teaches at a university.

I especially related to this article because I am of the same age and have also tried, for well over a decade now in this country, to "make it." Although I am from a privileged background, as a White male from Eu-rope, the way I feel about my experience is very similar. I can feel the power, I experience the fear, the constant need to compromise, because, af-ter all, I need to put food on the table for my kids, so better not make too many waves. . . . To hell with this kind of thinking! I feel so much better and affirmed in my decision now to go back to school and to slowly move away from a career in business, where no accomplishment is ever big enough anyway. (White, male)

In the following excerpt, a White woman shows her understanding of the class and her own process in becoming aware of privilege. She devel-ops a distinction between being a nonracist person and an antiracist person.

A nonracist person is how I would define myself before I took your class. I had no race consciousness but I had no problem with people of another race. I was conscious of the underprivileged status of people of color, but I was not conscious of my privileges as a White person. I was very con-scious of the racism that divides the American society, but felt that as a for-eigner I was not part of the American racism.

An antiracist person is much more proactive. An antiracist person is aware of the existence of the underprivileged and is also conscious of the people who have privileges. An antiracist is aware that the society is de-signed by and for the privileged and dominant group. An antiracist, after understanding the mechanism of the society, is willing to destroy the sys-tem and change it. (White, female)

Finally, a female student discusses how she has taken her privileged status for granted, including immunity from the daily strife of racism.

The book by Louis Stalvey did teach me about White privilege. It taught me that because I am White and have always been that I have taken many things for granted. I have never had any problems trying to rent an apart-ment. I have never been denied access to a restaurant, a club, a grocery store, a department store, or anywhere else because of the color of my skin. I have access to the best schools, the higher paying jobs (although I am still a woman, which limits the pay); I can be whatever I want. I received only support from my teachers throughout the year. I was never told I was stupid, but when I needed help with math, I was immediately given a tutor to assist me in developing the needed skills. I never had to worry about being in a neighborhood past dark. When I had encounters with the police for speeding, I did not have to worry that they would beat the shit out of me, or shoot me. I am, and always was, able to sit anywhere on the bus that I wanted to. I had the privilege of not having to deal with any of this racism on a daily basis. (White, female)

## IV. BECOMING AWARE OF SELF-INVOLVEMENT

Another step towards eradicating racism is to become aware that it exists in each one of us. None of us has escaped the painter; the forums of exposure may just be different. It is through fostering a deep level of self-awareness that our students began to face and question their own racist attitudes and beliefs for the first time in their lives. This is a scary yet truly empowering experience that many students reflected on. In this first excerpt, a White female faced her stereotypes about Latinos and realized that she painted them as somehow inferior.

> In the film "500 Years of Chicano History," I was able to identify with the White American majority saying, "You don't belong here. You can stay as long as we need you but then get out." The realization hurt me deeply. I have worked in restaurants where the kitchen crews were all Mexican. I laughed with them, enjoyed their company, tried to speak Spanish with them, and tried to understand their English. And all the while, I unknowingly saw them as inferior. I simply do not understand my own duplicity. I genuinely enjoyed their company and liked them, but I never respected their culture. I feel like I should go back and apologize to them. (White, female)

In the next example, a White female describes how she was always able to maintain her "White perspective." Her own version of a privileged reality maintained because she dismissed the stories of racism that students and friends had shared with her.

> I've been learning to be more introspective, and the results are less than desirable. To date, my biggest discovery is that I didn't really believe that people were being discriminated against because of their race. I could hear them say it, but in my head, I kept running a parallel reason from the White perspective. A Chinese lady says that her party had to wait longer while Whites kept getting seated in front of them. I say, other people had made reservations. A Black man says that the receptionist was rude, and made him wait longer because he's Black. I say she had a bad day, and the person he was there to see was busy. A Puerto Rican couple says that the second they drove into Modesto (I think that's the town) a cop started tailing

them, and continued to do so until they reached their hotel, which they opted to drive right on by because they didn't feel safe. I say, there's nothing to be afraid of in Modesto, it's a nice little town. And surely the cop wasn't following you because you're Puerto Rican. I bet your hotel was on his way to the station. I know that for every story in which something bad happens to someone because of their race, I can counter it with a White interpretation. And while I was listening with a sympathetic ear, I silently continued to offer up alternative explanations, benign explanations that kept my world in equilibrium. (White, female)

Another White student examined her assumption that an African American man wanted money when he addressed her. She was forced to ask herself was this assumption based solely on his color.

Last weekend I was walking in Westwood when an African American man approached me. The first thing that entered my mind was that he was going to ask me for money when he really just wanted to know what time it was. My assumption really disturbed me and so I asked a friend who was with me if she had the same assumption, and she said she did. Ever since this incident, I have been wondering why I made the assumption that I made. Was it because I was in Westwood and had already been approached several times for money? Or maybe it was because of what he was wearing. But then again, maybe, just maybe, it was because of his skin color, and that is wrong. (White, female)

One of the most difficult challenges for many of the students was overcoming the positive stereotypes of Asian students. In this first example, a student began to recognize her "illusions." Naming something as false is a big step in moving towards a nonracist identity.

I realize I have labeled Asians in a certain way. Seeing them as all model minorities, very studious, competitive, stoic, cheap, and passive, etc. I really feel I have come a long way in the last 7 weeks to get beyond this labeling and stereotyping. I think this is because I have seen and interacted with a number of Asians in our class and my LTD group, and my leader's group. They have all failed to live up to my stereotypes, *none of* them fit this image, and I see tremendous diversity among them as human beings. I feel very grateful for this opportunity to look at my labeling of this group because it really bothered me. I think the interacting that I've done with the number of Asians in the class has been the most important, but also writing in (the journal) and exploring the issue has helped as well as the class readings. I think specific articles that had to do with Asian issues were very enlightening. I think the sheer irrationality I've witnessed throughout our readings, films, discussions, etc., has really helped me to question and be aware of my unconscious stereotypes which are really based on nothing when I deconstruct them, so I am better at seeing them for what they are . . . ILLUSIONS. . . . (White, female)

In this next example, a student described how contacts with other students in the class transformed her views of Asians as the "model minority."

> Although I have Asian American friends, I have to admit that I have found myself buying into the myth of the model minority. I'd nod my head when I would look at the front row of my classes and see three rows predominantly full of Asian students, assuming that Asian students in my classes were better students than me. It really does take personal experience to rid myself of my belief in this myth. It has taken this class, in which I have had the opportunity to read articles, and actual students saying, "no, it is not that way for me, and I feel pressured to conform to it," for me to be able to begin to challenge this myth in my head. So I would imagine that at some point, the fact that I did harbor those stereotypes could have affected people and perhaps perpetuated their feeling of "less-than" or as model minority "study nerds." (White, female)

# V. REACTIONS TO SEEING IT: GUILT, FEAR, AND ANGER

Any kind of self-awareness can be frightening. This is particularly true when it is the first time we are examining an issue about ourselves. No one wants to look deeply within and find that they have been harboring racist ideals, beliefs, and practices. But the sooner that we collectively face this dilemma, the sooner we might begin to do the work that will eventually help alleviate our need to oppress. For our students, this was the first time many of them had come face-to-face with their own internalized racism.

In the next passage, a White female addresses the issue of ignorance and the stand she has decided to take against it.

> Ignorance is truly bliss. At least, it was. To go day-by-day denying racism and oppression, to live each day refusing to watch or read the news in anxiety that I would learn even more negativity about society and the world, to be ignorant of my surrounding and environment was blissful. Although I am aware of certain stereotypes that still currently hold, awareness is the first step to eradication. Life is harder once one becomes aware and conscious. Like the naive child, the unknowing and blinded individual sees no evil and hears no evil, yet evil is abounded. I know now that with my knowledge, with my awareness, I have a responsibility to act accordingly. I have to spread this seed planted within me. If I opt not to, I am no better than the racist. Being nonracist means taking an active stance against racism. (White, female)

This process of soul searching provokes the natural reaction of fear. However, it may do much more than that. It may inspire movement beyond fear, which can generate change within oneself and interactions with others.

After realizing his own racism, a White male comes to believe that he must take responsibility for his racism.

Awareness also brings responsibility. It is my responsibility, as well as others', to tell family, friends, relatives, and strangers about confronting racism and prejudice, instead of running away from them the way I did for quite awhile. I feel that I have a responsibility to tell these people, it is a part of my job, now that I know what lies ahead of them; I would have to spread the awareness about how racism and prejudice may be harmful to oneself if it is not faced. It will consume you from the inside out as it did me when I avoided the confrontation. I was unhappy and unsatisfied with always trying to hide behind a wall nonchalantly. (White, male)

In the following example, a White student questions what he would have done back in the days of Jim Crow laws. Though he is concerned that he would have been apathetic, he also begins to examine what active role he can play presently to fight racism.

I am pretty upset right now from the reading. . . . I feel so horrible from the persecution that Richard Wright felt, described, lived through, and how he was forced into submission into Jim Crow ways. I read without any awareness of time or page numbers. I was immersed in his terrifying world. About half way through I felt that I couldn't take anymore. I wasn't able to cry and I wasn't able to pretend that it was not true. I felt like I didn't know how to be. I was numb, ashamed, guilty, and scared. I endured reading the rest, as Wright had to endure his struggle his whole life. I can't believe the suffering of so many people in this world. It is so painful. It breaks me up and destroys my spirit and faith in the human race. What would I have done if I were alive and White back then (or even today in the Deep South or any place for that matter where deep, overt racism occurs)? Would I have helped Blacks even though I would have faced ostracism, and probably violence or death myself? Would I have been as racist and violent as the rest? . . . How do I live my life awake from here on in? How can I live my life with the courage to be willing to die so that I never tolerate being so inhuman or allowing others to be inhuman as well? To not allow such forms of overt racism to exist. As Freire says, how can I get it that I am not nor ever will be free if one of my brothers is suffering on the planet? What do I do? (White, male)

Another student explicitly states that awareness is scary. However, she begins to face the harsh reality that racism is commonplace for many students who have expressed their pain in class.

I have a fear of speaking as a member of the dominant group, being ¾ White. My feelings of fear stem from not wanting to be labeled as being a racist. I think that fear also stems from the inner fear that I do not want to know what happens to people of color everyday. I may not directly be a racist, but not reacting or speaking up to try to change things is a result of my guilt. By doing this journal we are asked to look inside ourselves. This is a frightening prospect because I do not want to see the possibility that I have been a racist. Awareness is scary. I take for granted my Whiteness, not wanting to accept that racism is commonplace, but it must be so because the others [in the class] have shown examples and [shared] anecdotes. (Biracial, White-Mexican, female)

Another student shares that becoming aware of her White privilege has frightened her. But attached to her fear are the beginning questions of change.

Now that I know and am conscious about White privilege, what do I do? When it boils down to it, I am scared. What would my life be like without White privilege? I have no desire to have a privilege that only Whites can *to* enjoy, but I do like having privilege. This I will not deny. (White, female)

In this next example, a White student comes to question his passivity towards racism. He realizes that his laissez-faire stance was ineffective and unacceptable. Racism is now about a struggle that he will actively address.

I used to feel that if I just do my thing, don't discriminate, that I've done my part and nothing more is needed. I used to think that I am only responsible for myself and for no one else. How could I be part of the problem? It's not my fight. After thinking about it, I am realizing it is my fight. I am responsible . . . that's why if I'm not part of the solution, I am like all those who have gone before me and done nothing [about racism]. (Irish American, male)

On a very poignant note, one student ponders about friendships that never developed. He described how he was always waiting for the "other" to approach him. He was afraid to make a mistake, so he never attempted to reach out in order to understand other races and cultures.

I feel like I have lost so many possible friendships because I was never able to look past those labels before . . . Like the Black man said in the "Color of Fear," I was always waiting for the "other" to come to me. Afraid to make a mistake, not willing to take a step, I have lost many potential friends. I do not expect others to emulate me; rather I realize that it is time I made the first step (in terms of trying to understand another's race and culture). (White, male)

In the next statement, a White student reflects on how his ignorance caused him to be blind to the pain of racism. His new-found awareness causes him to realize that he can never go back to pretense.

In the movie "The Color of Fear" I found myself watching David [a White male] and cringing. What he was saying were things I have said. His beliefs were beliefs that I have held. That is who I was before I took this class.

I was ignorant to what was going on around me, just like David. I was blind to the pain. I did not want to accept the truth. Now I can never be blind to it; it will always be with me. (White, female)

# VI. CHANGE

Transforming identities, changing beliefs, dropping assumptions and stereotypes, and intervening to stop oppression are extremely difficult tasks. Recognizing that we are all racist and that we are all implicated in racism is a fundamental step in the process of attaining a nonracist identity. We all have had moments when we wanted to say something, stand up for someone, do something and we did nothing. No one is clean. We have been taught to paint and we all have painted. When White people hear about the sins of the past and the present and find out that many of their race have acted as oppressors, they often feel hurt by their lack of awareness.

> I had gone to the dentist's office for a checkup and I was filling out my paperwork, I saw an African American lady with a white doctor's coat come into the reception area and call out my name, She was the new dental assistant the office had hired. For a second I panicked. I thought to myself, 'I have never seen her before . . . she's new . . . what if she is not capable of doing her job right . . . what if she doesn't have enough experience. Maybe I should ask for the doctor?' Then, right in the middle of my thought process I stopped and asked myself, "is there any reason why you're doubting her capabilities?" the answer was NO. Then I asked myself, "Would you be this apprehensive if she was White?" the answer was no, again. At that moment I realized I was undermining the value of this very intelligent and sophisticated lady based on the color of her skin. I was reacting based on my racist, socialized beliefs. Right there and then I stopped myself. I closed my eyes for a second. When I opened them again, I looked into her face and truly saw this beautiful African American lady for who she is rather than the color of her skin. (White, female)

However, our students' voices indicated that our class provided them with some of the ammunition and tools necessary to begin to examine and question their painting instructors.

> Thus, I have begun by acknowledging that I am separate, distinct, and readily identify with all of my cultures and complex experiences, according to my own definitions, not the profiled existence everyone else expects. (Multiracial, female)

Moreover, these students have looked at themselves as painters and found that they did not like what they were painting. In the following, a woman refutes the idea that it is a compliment to be called a good White person.

But I do not like the way White is defined as a nonethnic group just because it is mainstream or has been dominant. It is not any better than any other group nor is it any worse. Every ethnicity has importance and worthy ideals. Each group has something great that it can contribute to American culture. I also want to change the perception of White people. I want to try to be a reverse Oreo. I don't want people to call me a good White person. I should not have to be praised for not having racial prejudices and for being open-minded and tolerant. (White, female)

More importantly, not only have the students begun to acknowledge that they have internalized prejudice and hate, but that they have also thought about ways to change their negative stereotypes and racist behaviors. In the next example, a student understands that the job of dismantling racism falls more heavily upon Whites than people of color.

I believe myself to be a strong individual, and the more I learn about myself, the stronger I become. Because I am White, I feel that it is my duty to fight the hardest because it is White people who have the most history of oppressing others. For reasons such as these, and because I am a woman who knows what it is like to be sexually oppressed, I pledge to continue in this process of learning and understanding so as to help raise my own consciousness, as well as the consciousness of society. (White, female)

Sometimes the decision to change oneself is more localized. A Latina sees her new-found changes as something that will help generations that follow her.

All I can do is change myself and raise my children to love and respect all people. By changing myself and raising my children properly, I am helping out society for generations to come. (Latina, female)

Many of our students have begun to put down their paintbrushes and are letting their canvas dictate their art instead of the other way around. Sometimes speaking up can be a way of promoting nonracist behavior. In the following example, a woman of color describes how her new "voice" has allowed her to intervene at a local dance club.

My voice became more prominent, as I would be sure to make myself heard whenever I felt an injustice was being done. I went to a club one night, and a light-skinned Black young lady was in the restroom making a fuss over how dark skinned the men were, calling them such atrocities as "crispy" and "burnt," and wondering aloud why they didn't "just go back to Africa where they came from." I shook my head at her and told her "shame on you," and asked her how she would feel if someone said that about her parents; two other girls similarly chided in. She dismissed my comment and said she was just drunk, and not to mind her. As she bounced out of the bathroom, several of the females looked at each other in awe and made comments about how they couldn't believe people like that. I was proud of myself, I was proud that I initiated such a debate, I was proud that I (unlike the other females in the restroom) spoke my mind in the face of a conflict. I was proud that I incorporated the concepts I was exposed to in the classroom. (Asian, female)

A few of the students in the class were older. These nontraditional students had families and were raising children and had now returned to school. In this next excerpt, a parent models nonracist behavior to a couple who are her close friends as well as to her children. The discussion occurs during her family's evening meal.

My social circle is composed of predominantly White and privileged people. One day, I was discussing with my daughter's best friend's mother as to why I enrolled my children at the Lycee Francais School. It is a school that allows my children to be educated in French, my native language. I told this woman that if it were not for the French, I would have probably put my children into the local high school, Pacific Palisades. After all, my husband went to the same high school and was later accepted at UCLA. My friend said, "I would never consider putting my daughter into a public school. My children would be mixed with inner-city Black and Latino children. How will you react when your daughter has a Black boyfriend? I want my daughter to grow up with her peers" (she meant White children). Although I disagreed with what she said, I remained silent and decided that in the future I was going to avoid her as much as I could. We stayed "civil" to each other, mainly because of the indestructible friendship that bonded our daughters.

Recently, my husband and I had dinner with that woman and her husband. I was describing how one day my daughter came with me to my class to watch a documentary about Jane Elliott's "blue eyes, brown eyes experiment." After seeing the documentary, my daughter noted that in her class, there was a Black little girl who was not liked by her peers and the teacher "because she didn't work well and because she is too noisy. The teacher screams at her but she doesn't listen." My daughter understood that the treatment toward the Black little girl was because the teacher didn't like her and that the children in the class didn't like her as well.

As I finished my story to the couple, I noticed how I gained their attention. They became very quiet. Then the father asked me how it was possible to get the cassette of Jane Elliott's experiment, as he wanted his own children to watch it. (White, female)

A Latino describes the isolation that he felt prior to the class and the struggles he made towards achieving a nonracist identity.

As I review the way I've changed as a result of this class, I have realized that the hardest parts for me dealt with many of my own demons. I had grown up in a predominantly White neighborhood, so talking with dominants was not something I found terribly difficult. As one can imagine, though, I didn't often pass the time discussing racial issues with many of my White friends. However, at times I felt more at ease with them than with "my own." Because of where I grew up, how I spoke, and how I acted, I have always been considered the sell-out, the White-washed Mexican. Consequently, I grew up in a state of racial confusion. Other Latinos did not accept me, yet as I unconsciously internalized the dominant view of myself as a person of color, I still could not completely embrace my White neighbors either. Before taking this course I had no idea that others thought or felt the same way I did. When I first heard someone in class echoes a thought or belief or even expresses confusion like my own, I felt I had found a new family. I thought that I had finally found people that I might be able to relate to, to talk with, to help me through all of the tough questions I was beginning to ask about myself. Most importantly, I had found others I could simply dialogue with and help muddle through our racial identification process together. Finding just one class like this at UCLA has made my academic career more fulfilling than I had ever possibly imagined.

This course has helped me to find a voice. But before I can have a meaningful dialogue with others, I first have to deal with my own inner turmoil. I never realized all that I take for granted. I have learned so much that I have never questioned—things about myself, as well as about other groups. I look at the labels that I use, the way I view myself; I try to question everything now. I see that no one is free from this racial internalization. (Latino, male)

In this last excerpt a White female describes how she was educated to believe that great progress has been made in race relations in America. Her shock and surprise is that for many people of color, racism is still a major factor in their lives. At the age of 20 she has become aware of the salience of racism and the significance of privilege for many White Americans.

When an event of racial or social inequality was mentioned, it was taught in a very cut-and-dry, absolutely historical sense. Good thing Harriet Tubman led some slaves to freedom; good thing Lincoln fixed the South of its morally misguided affinity for slavery; good thing that's all behind us now. With that in the past, we can finally live as equals as just humans. Race is taught as a nonissue. Imagine my surprise when it was made clear to me that for some people, namely non-Whites, race is an issue. And now I'm starting to learn why, 20 years too late. (White, female)

# STUDENT TESTIMONIALS

After reading the various entries in *Voices of Pain and Voices of Hope,* I was reminded of the times that I have gone on strict diets to lose weight, highlighted my hair with blond streaks. I also had an intense desire to wear green contacts, so as to resemble the girls depicted on the cover of magazines! Moving to America was quite an experience for me. Given that I was fair with light brown eyes, I was always complimented and fawned upon as a child, while my sister was always referred to as the darker one and even "darkie." However, as I grew older I tanned and my eyes have gotten darker leading to much distress amongst the female members of my family! I grew more aware of South Asian females who would often stay in for fear that they will become "dark." Hence it was quite an epiphany when I began to understand the motivation behind my behavior as well as that of my family.

**Rubaiyat Karim, Bangali/South Asian, Female, Graduate, California State University, Northridge**

In reading *Voices of Pain and Voices of Hope* I became aware of many new things and aware of the prevalence of other things I already knew existed. As a White person I was already aware of the privilege that exists for me on a daily basis and as a White person with a multiracial family, I was acutely aware of the fact that not everyone has those privileges and that the dominants in our society can revoke your privilege whenever they feel you have misused it. But even as a person with this experience and knowledge I have to admit that I was blind to the concept of the paintbrush.

I myself was guilty in the past of naively thinking that the solution may lie in everyone behaving, talking, and dressing the same. I thought this out of desperate attempts to want to fix the racism that I knew was out there; but as a White person of course when I thought this I always thought about everyone behaving, talking, and dressing like me. Prior to this book I had come to understand the concept of different realities and I knew from having a biracial family the importance of having images that look like your child around them. But until *Voices,* I did not understand the paintbrush and its prevalence in our society. I was shocked and dismayed to read from these students the amount of painting that had been done to them and by them up to this point. I also found a little irony in the fact that so many people had put time into trying to paint these students to be someone like me when they had achieved acceptance into a prestigious university that I, a White privileged dominant, had not done well enough to get in to. Reading excerpts from the journals of the bi- and multiracial students was very informative for me. As a parent of a biracial child I know that I always make sure that she has toys that look like her, and that we watch shows with people who look like her, and that I always try to represent both sides of who she is. I was touched by the student who wrote that her mother (who was White) did not teach her about the fact that she would be perceived as a person of color and of the ramifications that had on her as she got older. This was very important for me. Since my daughter was small I have had her watch movies about Martin Luther King and the civil rights struggle and I have not hesitated to make comments about racist people and what they do and what that means. Others have told me that I should not subject her to this and that I am ignoring the fact that she is White when I do this. I now feel that I have done the right thing, it is clear from these students in *Voices* that it does not matter if part of her is White, she is a person of color and her experiences will be of such. Because of that, I am so thankful that I have been given this marvelous tool by Maria Root (The Bill of Rights for Multi-Cultural People) that I can share with my daughter to help foster in her a strong foothold to the individual she chooses to be. From this book I have felt renewed strength to help others let go of the guilt, fear, and anger that comes from thinking and knowing about racism and do what I can to help White people understand the difference between being nonracist and antiracist. Most of all, I would like to wash away the white paint, wherever I may see it.

**Jennifer Odum, White, Female, Sociology Major, California State University, Northridge**

I am a White, Jewish female from Belgium, and I had to read *Voices of Pain and Voices of Hope* in the first class I ever took at UCLA.

The frank and open testimonies from students of this book helped me to understand the reasons for some of my difficulties of integrating to American society. They made me notice that some obstacles that I had to overcome, as a foreigner, were similar to those imposed on American minority students. It also made me understand that my White skin helped a great deal in my process to overcome those obstacles, while for people of color, those similar obstacles would most likely remain permanent.

Secondly, *Voices* provided me with valuable insights on how American people look at each other through the lens of race. It warned me of learning the culture of my adoptive country with discernment because it would be very easy for a foreigner, like me, to learn, along with a new culture and a new language, beliefs and attitudes conducive to racism. *Voices* taught me to detect and discriminate racist and nonracist attitudes.

Finally, and most importantly, this book made me question my own attitudes and beliefs toward minority people from my native country. I already knew that racism exists in every nation. By reading *Voices*, I became aware that I had similar beliefs towards minority people from my own country, North African people. Many words spoken by students of color in this book could have been palced in the mouths of people of non-European background living in Belgium.

I am now majoring in Political Science at UCLA, with a specialization in International Politics. Reading *Voices* has helped me to remember that too often decisions in international affairs never took— and still do not take into account people's individual sufferings. Testimonies from this book undeniably demonstrate that regardless of skin color, ethnic background, languages, or culture, the pain is felt the same way for everyone.

**Nathalie Polakoff, White, Jewish, Female from Belgium, Honors Student, University of California, Los Angeles**

As a man of science, I've always placed my faith in numbers. Their objectivity gave me the solace that through them I could understand life impartially. This was the mentality that I held before entering the class. What I needed to convince me that racism existed was something that quantified it that proved its existence.

What I realized after reading *Voices of Pain, Voices of Hope* was that racism is not a phenomenon that can be directly quantified. It's impossible to survey people being racist because their actions and thoughts often do not coincide. The most loving people are capable of racism, and not because they wanted to, but because racism is bred into their mentality. Racism exists in the interaction between two or more persons, and just as these interactions can have subtle undertones, racism can be subtle.

Racism's subtlety blinded me for a long time as well. For a long time I didn't believe that I had ever encountered any racist acts or remarks, but *Voices* showed me otherwise. Its testimonials showed me that I was not only a victim but a perpetrator of racism. I've committed many of the "crimes" in the testimonials, but I've also been victim to many as well.

All in all, *Voices* has enlightened me in many ways. It has given me a better perspective of what racism is, allowed me to see its many different forms, and even given me a better perspective of myself.

**Jimmy Yang, Taiwanese American, University of California, Los Angeles Graduate**

Reading *Voices of Pain, Voices of Hope* forced me to fully take hold of an identity that I thought I already owned. Being a Sikh female is something I always "thought" I took pride in, but after reading this book I had to reevaluate my self worth. Turbans, long flowing beards, and traditional Indian wardrobe are part of my everyday life, yet the white ideal stood a close second. Meshing the two worlds was an unknown goal of mine, begging my mom to not wear traditional clothes outside the house, trying to teach my uncle to pronounce words without an accent, or asking him to wear a smaller less noticeable turban. Reading this book was a wake up call for me because I realized that the pride I used to take in being Sikh and Indian was on a daily basis being washed away by standards set by those unlike me. Reading *Voices* helped me to set a standard within myself to not only accept what I am but to embrace who I am.

**Sonia Joat, Punjabi Sikh, Female, Graduate, California State University, Northridge**

# VII

## America's New Paintbrush*— But Also Old

### With the assistance of
Rubaiyat Karim

*Chapter Seven is a new addition to this second edition of this book. Because there has been such an outpouring of hatred, prejudice and discrimination towards Middle Eastern and South Asian students since 9/11, I felt that their voices needed to be included and heard.*

Since the events of September 11, 2001, our American government and many of its citizens have found a seemingly new target for their prejudice, discrimination, hatred, and even murder. We have turned on our fellow citizens and deprived them of their basic civil rights, their livelihoods, and their feelings of safety and security. Many of the Middle Eastern and South Asian parents of these students are newly arrived immigrants to this country. They have come here with the hope for a better life, with a desire for freedom, and with admiration in their hearts for the United States. However, religious and ethnic profiling has made it very difficult for them to

---

*The following chapter includes student voices from other campuses besides UCLA. Professor Rabow has been teaching at California State University, Northridge, where a large group of Middle Eastern and South Asian students pursue their education. He has heard and learned much from them. Their experiences should illustrate the new form of painting that is sweeping our nation. Part racism, part religious condemnation this is the new pain for many young American men and women who are different. The students you will be hearing from had many friends in the Southern California area who also wanted to make their stories known. Thus, the voices you read will be from California State University Northridge, University California Los Angeles, and University of Southern California.

continue to love this country in the ways that they had. Just as members of any one ethnic group are often considered to look alike, Middle Eastern and South Asians are also seen as not only looking alike but also as belonging to the same religion. Although Middle Eastern and South Asian people can be Buddhist, Christian, Catholic, Hindu, Jain, and Jewish, they are often lumped together as Muslims. And this religion is now considered by many Americans as inferior and as one that poses a major threat to our way of life. Americans should not think, however, that this all started with the events of September 11th. Middle Eastern and South Asian students and their families have long been subject to discrimination, prejudice, and stereotypes. An Armenian-Iraqi male describes his experiences in public school prior to the attacks on the Twin Towers and the Pentagon by Al-Queda. This young child's father goes beyond the standard advice that newly arrived immigrants give to their children about the importance of assimilation. His father's words communicate to his son the fear that Americans will know that his son is an Iraqi.

> When I was in the fifth or sixth grade, my dad told me before I went to school that I shouldn't tell anyone that I am Iraqi. When I asked him as to the reasons for concealing my identity he responded by stating that he was afraid of what would happen to me. With this in mind, I disassociated myself with my culture. I was against Iraq and in support of America in fear that something would happen to me if I slipped and said something. I was afraid of telling people who I was. When I told people that I was Armenian American (disassociating myself from my Iraqi heritage), I felt that I had betrayed myself for a country that betrayed me.

The basis for his father's fears went back to the Gulf War. This student was protected from the knowledge of what had happened to his family prior to September 11th. It was only after September 11th that the student found out about his family's experience during the Gulf War. The student is able to identify with another historical event in American racism, the internment of Japanese Americans in World War II.

> Upon speaking to my mother, I learned that a similar situation had occurred during the Gulf War. Upon placing the house under surveillance for months, FBI agents had informed my father that they had concluded that we seemed "good" and did not seem to pose any type of threat to national security. When I heard this, I was blown away. The FBI placed me under surveillance merely because I am Iraqi. I began to understand the plight of the Japanese American during World War II. (Armenian-Iraqi, male, California State University Northridge)

A Pakistani female was less fortunate in being able to hide her identity. She describes her pre-September 11th life as a series of experiences that made her feel like an outcast.

As a hijabi Muslim, I am certainly accustomed to the stares and comments: the discomfort of having to walk into a room and be greeted by the cold stares of every individual in that room was not a novel experience for me. (Pakistani, female, University of Southern California, Masters in Accountancy, 2002)

Occasionally, adults who are responsible for the care and well-being of children seek to teach and educate others about difference. In a pre-September 11th story, a young man was supported by his teacher to do a presentation on his country of origin. It would be hard to imagine that educators could sponsor these programs throughout the United States in 2004.

Luckily for me, I got a chance to show people I was Iraqi. In sixth grade, my teacher asked us to create a presentation on the country of our origin. I had to the option of joining the group of Armenians or making up my own group for Iraqis. I was alone. The first time I told the class that I was doing my presentation on Iraq, everyone looked at me differently. I felt like I was coming out of the closet but the closet was locked. While working on the presentation and painting the Iraqi flag, I was bombarded with malicious looks, cruel remarks like "sand nigger," and odd questions such as "Are you related to Saddam?" Fewer children played with me during recess but I was glad that I still had my friends who looked past my culture. Finally, the day came when I had to do my presentation in front of hundreds of students. Before we went out, my teacher announced to the class, "I'm very proud of A for doing his presentation on Iraq. It's a very brave thing to do. Everyone give him a round of applause." I gave a halfway smile not knowing if it was a good or bad thing. The time came and everyone got up to the podium and discussed their culture. Countries that were well known received much applause from the students. When I did my presentation, I only received applause from a tenth of the students. I remember I looked up at one moment while I was reading my presentation and I saw faces that were amazed that an Iraqi was in their school. (Armenian-Iraqi, male, California State University Northridge)

The events of September 11th paralyzed many Americans. While some felt lost and frightened, others felt a desire for revenge and for attacking Al-Queda. Our students also reported feelings of fear, helplessness, and confusion. The daily rhythm of their lives had been disrupted and they were lost because they were being labeled.

The time following the 9/11 attacks was an awkward period in my life. I didn't know what to do. I didn't know what to say. I am an Armenian-Iraqi American, who was being labeled a "terrorist" in my own country. (Armenian-Iraqi, male, California State University Northridge)

A Pakistani female student was so concerned for her safety could not continue her life as a student. She predicted the events that were going to take place in our country after the attacks on September 11th. Her concerns, however, extend beyond the name-calling and labeling she is subjected to. She is also concerned regarding her physical safety. Surprisingly, her peers challenge her for her concerns.

> Following the attacks on the World Trade Center, I confined myself to my apartment. I refused to go to classes or to a store for bare essentials for I was extremely concerned for my safety. I was certain that hate crimes and bias against hijabi Muslim would rise exponentially due to the terrorist attacks. Amazingly though, a few of my friends chastised me for being a recluse, stating that by refraining from partaking in my daily activities I would be allowing the ignorant people to win. Easier said than done. I am the one who asked if there was bomb in my backpack. I am the one greeted by comments such as "I hope she doesn't blow the place up" when I enter an ice-cream shop. I was the one flipped off by strangers. I am the one who was called Saddam. I am the one who was refused service when I attempted to purchase a watch from a major department store in Northridge. I am the one who causes a 21-year-old Caucasian female to request a change of seating on an airplane. I am the one who was kept waiting when I went to dine at a restaurant. I am the one that is the target of all "patriots." I AM the one who is treated as evil and inferior EVERYDAY. (Pakistani, female, University of Southern California, Masters in Accountancy, 2002)

The *New York Times* in an article printed only one week after the attacks confirms the concern expressed by the Pakistani woman. According to the *Times* (2001), "since the attacks, people who look Middle Eastern and South Asian, whatever their religion or nation of origin, have been singled out . . ." These acts have included arson, harassment, assaults, hate speech, airline/airport discrimination, employment discrimination, and murder. The American-Arab Anti-Discrimination Committee also reported receiving messages which included: "You f****** Arabs, go to hell. You will pay . . ." "ROT IN HELL FOREVER," "The only good Arab is a dead one," and "You people are animals . . . I feel sick to my stomach to see an Arab." Our students therefore represent the experiences of Middle Eastern, South Asian, and Muslim citizens. A report by the FBI shows an increase of 1,600% in hate crimes and bias incidents committed against individuals of Middle Eastern and South Asian descent by the civic population as well as a series of administrative directives from the government.[1]

The ripples of this event began entering into the world of personal and intimate relationships. In the following excerpt a Sri-Lankan female is confronted and accused by her boyfriend. Although they have been together

---

[1]Bakalian, A., & Bozorgmehr, M. *Discriminatory reactions to September 11th, 2001 terrorism. Encyclopedia of Racism in the United States.* Westport, CT: Greenwood Press.

for a year and a half, her boyfriend cannot believe that his girlfriend was opposed to the Al-Queda attacks. He refuses to recognize the possibility of a Muslim who is extremely upset by the attacks on America. He cannot accept her grief about the possibility that she herself may have lost friends in the Twin Tower attacks. Ironically, he was an individual who himself had known prejudice and persecution and who now is turning on his own girlfriend in a way that subordinates sometimes turn on and blame other subordinates. Even her religious practices, which he had never commented upon during their relationship, are belittled and insulted. This young man is unable to comprehend that Muslims might be going to a mosque to pray rather than to plan attacks on America. The young woman also predicts the rise of future anti-Muslim and anti-South Asian behavior.

> September 13th, 2001 will forever remain engraved in my mind. The unfortunate events that occurred a few days before were the topic of the conversation with my boyfriend, who I had been with for about a year and a half. I was overwhelmed by sorrow given that I had friends and relatives who lived in the area surrounding the World Trade Center who were still unaccounted for. After speaking about the matter for a while, my boyfriend asked me how I felt about regarding the attacks. I responded by reiterating that I was horrified and extremely empathic to the families of the victims; emotions that paralleled those of most individuals in the country. My boyfriend DID NOT SEEM quite satisfied OR CONVINCED by my response—his contention being that since I was Muslim, much like the terrorists who flew the airplanes into the Twin Towers, I must identify with their cause. I defended my position quite vehemently and he conceded. However, he went on to question what my parents thought a propos of the attacks. He was quite adamant in his belief about my parents. He said that he could understand that I might not condone the actions of the terrorists because I was partially raised in the United States. He was, however, quite sure that my conservative Muslim parents were in support of the terrorist cells in some form or manner. Once again, I repeated that they were stunned and horrified by the harrowing event. However, he questioned as to what they "really" thought about the attacks as if to suggest that we support the acts in silence for fear of reprisal from the U.S. government. I was enraged that my African American boyfriend, who was quite active in fighting racism and prejudice in the African American community, would be so incredibly ignorant as to associate the acts committed by the terrorists to my spiritual beliefs.
>
> UNFORTUNATELY, that conversation served as a microcosm of the gamut of events that would occur in the months to come. Suffice to say, my relationship did not last for long—not only was he quite firm in his belief that Muslims around the country endorsed the terrorists, he would also make derogatory comments such as referring to the Friday prayer at the mosque as the "weekly meeting for terrorists." This experience made me

feel uneasy about who I am not because I had taken part in an atrocious act but merely because I had chosen to adhere to Islam. (Sri-Lankan, female, University of Southern California, 2003)

Another fissure occurs in close peer relations in high school. This break in friendship occurred between a Jewish student and her close Muslim friends. Prior to September 11th, this student describes her high school friendships as ones that celebrated diversity. Muslim and Jewish holidays were discussed and friendships were based upon appreciation of these differences. All this was transformed after September 11th. A rift is created when racial slurs and jokes are introduced into the peer group relationships. Her feelings of respect for others who are different are transformed into feelings of fear, anger, and even hatred. Three years after the estrangement, she is still struggling with a set of feelings that she is not comfortable with. She confesses that she is embarrassed by her newfound racism.

In high school, I had many Muslim Persian American, and Jewish American friends. Between all of us, religion had only been talked about in terms of our different and interesting customs and holidays. But that all changed in my senior year of 2001 when the Twin Towers were targeted. Soon, my big eclectic group of friends split right down to a group of Jewish friends and Muslim friends. The split only occurred after religious jokes and hatred surfaced about one another. And today, three years after 9/11, as deeply as this saddens me to say, I look back and think about how I could have even befriended Muslims in the first place. I hate this feeling of my new-found racism; I had never before thought badly of Muslims and have always hated generalizations about any group of people, but I cannot help this feeling. (Jewish, female, University of California Los Angeles, 2004)

Public events, which our students attend to enjoy themselves, can also become places that create painful experiences for Middle Eastern and South Asian students. In the following excerpt a Pakistani student embarks upon an all-day event at UCLA. She goes with her roommate, who was planning to meet her boyfriend at the festival. This encounter between the Pakistani woman and roommate's boyfriend leads to the quick departure of her boyfriend and his friends for they became frightened upon seeing the hijab that the student wore. This experience with false accusations and name-calling is one of the many experiences that remind her that the word "Muslim" is immediately associated with the word "terrorist" by many Americans.

In the summer of 2002, I attended the UCLA Jazz Festival with my roommate. Upon arrival, we met up with her Ethiopian boyfriend, who was also there with his friends. However, things did not go as planned for soon after we all met, her boyfriend wanted to leave. Perplexed, she simply said goodbye and we continued to enjoy the festival. It was only later that night that we discovered the reasons as to his quick departure. You see I am a hijabi (veiled) Muslim and this caused quite a lot of discomfort among his friends for I could be a "suicide bomber." My roommate was quite upset that he could fall prey to such ignorant beliefs especially since 45% of Ethiopians are Muslim. Her boyfriend and his friends had refused to stay at the Jazz Festival for fear that I might be a suicide bomber. This is only one event in an array of many that serves to remind me that Muslims are oft associated with such terms as "zealots," "terrorist," and "militants." Every time I enter a room, I am reminded that my identity is the cause of much discomfort for many via suspicious glances, whispered comments and gawps. It has become a constant struggle to prove that you are not like "them" (terrorists). (Pakistani, female, University of California Los Angeles, 2002)

The rupture of peer relations, though very disturbing and painful, is perhaps less critical than issues of employment. In the following excerpt a Persian student reports how frightened she was to return to her regular place of employment. Her parents, who also express their fears to her, compound her fears. Her parents have been inundated with reports from various friends of the family who were being intimidated. This student is confronted with the dilemma that almost all of our Middle Eastern and South Asian students had to deal with. They wore clothing and religious symbols that were significant representations of who they were. These symbols became the stimulus for attacks. She returns to work with a strategy for minimizing potential attacks. Unfortunately, this strategy fails. A customer complains to a manager about their employment of such people. The woman is unable to respond to her attacker and unfortunately her frustration is aimed at herself and her people rather than the attacker.

After I returned to work, I maintained minimum amount of contact with my coworkers for fear that one of them would ask me: "So does Islam teach Muslims to be terrorists?" However, that question came from a customer that I was serving a week after the attacks. A middle-aged, Caucasian woman whom I was helping noticed my pendant and proceeded to question me as to its meaning. It so happened that I was wearing a pendant that said Allah (God) in Arabic. She became quite irate and began to spew a plethora of hateful comments. I was flabbergasted at first for although I had expected it I was never prepared to respond to her comments. I had not prepared a response because a part of me believed what she was saying. A part of me was ashamed of my religion and my people. The woman refused to be served by me and informed my manager that she ought to be ashamed of herself for employing "such people!" (Persian, female, California State University Northridge, 2003)

The pre-September 11th treatment towards many Middle Eastern and South Asian Americans was mild compared to events immediately after

September 11th. However, the behavior of Americans towards Middle Eastern and South Asian Americans escalated in intensity. Being spit upon, cursed and yelled at, stabbed, having tires slashed, and receiving death threats became part of our American landscape. In the following excerpt, a Sri-Lankan female receives phone calls and e-mails from friends and family members from all parts of America, who are going to school in some of our leading universities. They describe their experiences with this new wave of hatred and persecution. Like the Persian female, this Sri-Lankan female begins to question her strongly held beliefs.

I began to receive e-mails and phone calls from friends and relatives from New York University, Stanford University, University of Pennsylvania, University of North Carolina Charlotte, University of Virginia, and George Washington University, who would relate to me the ridiculous questions they were asked by individuals who approached them on the premise of being "curious." As reports began to show an increasing number of casualties as well as fiscal loss, my friends and relatives had their tires slashed, their hijabi (veiled) sisters were spit at, their parents received death threats at their establishments, and they were made to feel LESS. I was made to feel as though being Muslim was innately "bad." I wondered, "Do I ascribe to a religion that teaches its believers hatred?" (Sri-Lankan, female, University of Southern California, 2003)

The attacks on our students do not always start with a condemnation, name-calling, or an accusation. Sometimes, it is the casual encounter in public, which begins with an innocent-sounding question that can quickly evolve into an attack that reveals the bigotry of the individual. In the following excerpt, an Iranian woman is confronted by a belief expressed by a man that is truly shocking.

As I stood in line at a coffee shop in Northridge, a White male of about 50 who stood before me struck up a conversation, which lead from a mundane discussion regarding the warm weather to his involvement with the Bush administration. I was curious and so I questioned him regarding his dealings with George W. Bush. He began to inform me as to what an amazing individual President George W. Bush is and emphasized his perception by stating that he was the only president to learn Spanish. Failing to understand the significance of such a gesture, I questioned him further regarding the matter and he explained that it was a means of establishing rapport with the Spanish-speaking communities in the United States of America. Still quite baffled, I informed him as to the absence of significant changes made by the administration to alleviate the unique struggles faced by the Latino community. Besides, given that he is the president of United States, he ought to be well versed not only in English but also in various languages so as to facilitate diplomatic relations. Irked, he stated, "Imagine what it would be like if he learned Ebonics, or worse yet Arabic. That would be equivalent to having a banner stating, 'All terrorists are welcome here.' Astounded by the man's utter bigotry, I walked away. I felt angry and hurt that people held such notions about Middle Eastern people. The incident crystallized the notion that the perceptions that arose regarding people of Middle Eastern descent in the aftermath of the attacks on 9/11 would not dissipate. Time and again, I was faced with individuals who were suspicious of Middle Eastern people and were eager to report "any suspicious activity." (Irani, female, University of California Los Angeles, 2003)

The difference in treatment by many Americans towards Muslim American citizens was drastically changed after September 11th. All of the students we have heard from report this difference. From cool reception to an occasional friendship, from genuine inquisitiveness and appreciation, there is now fear, anger, hostility, and hatred. One of our students, a Pakistani female, reflects on her experiences as a Muslim woman prior to September 11th with fondness. Although she was teased and made fun of, in retrospect these events seem almost benign.

As a young girl, I thought a hijab was cool and warranted by Islam, my way of life. During the Persian Gulf War, I was quite offended when other children would tease me incessantly and say, "Oh, there is one of Saddam's people." But now, after 9/11, it was the same teasing but with a different face: "Oh look there is one of Osama bin Laden's daughters!" I felt so hurt. Before 9/11, it had been a while since people had teased me; things were coming around in this country. Instead, people were opening up to the Muslims and asking lots of questions such as, "why do you wear the hijab?" But 9/11 made me feel as though we reverted to square one. It became a struggle once again. So many of my friends have been stopped at airports merely due to their "Islamic" look or name. On top of it all, we had to be more careful. My father didn't let me go to school on 9/11, fearing the people around us. My older brother and I were afraid to take any book with Arabic written on it. (Pakistani, female, University of California Los Angeles, 2004)

Most Americans, although annoyed, welcome the new security measures at the airports they use. However, most Americans are not subjected to the kind of examination that Middle Eastern and South Asian Americans have received. All of the students that you have heard from also reported how they themselves, their families, and their relatives are profiled at airports. In the following story, a South Asian male, who also appreciates the security provided at our airports, is made to realize that there is a new era of religious discrimination in America.

9/11 incidents were just as horrible for me as for any other American. But I never thought this incident would start a new era of religious discrimination and racism. Among many other precautionary measurements after 9/11, one is the higher security level at the airports. I always thought the higher security at the airport is for our own safety. However, it was only when I experienced racial profiling myself that I began to feel uncomfortable regarding the various security levels. I had traveled quite extensively prior to 9/11 without much ado; but after 9/11 for the first time I began to hate myself for being South Asian. I felt like an alien that is considered to be a danger to everyone around him. As I stood in the aisle to go through the detectors at Heathrow airport, the airport security officials approached me without any hesitation as though they have a certain criteria to select a passenger for a "random search." I was asked to take off my shoes, belt, jacket, hat, and even socks. The security officials also checked my passport and carry-on luggage. Although it might appear as though this is an isolated incident of a random search I am hard pressed to call it so given that I was selected for a "random search" four times on the same day and the same airport. (South Asian, male California State University Northridge)

Security and profiling are not the only forms of harassment that our student's experienced. There are also in-flight forms of prejudice and discrimination. In the following excerpt, a young Sikh is asked to sit in another part of the plane after he has boarded and sat down. This questioning from the flight attendant leads him to imagine how criminals feel. Of course, his criminal behavior is only a result of the way he dresses and looks.

Firstly, I must say that I am a baptized Sikh and when traveling anywhere I prefer to wear a round turban with my beard flowing. This has caused me a lot of problems in the past including being stopped at security checkpoints at airports and other such incidents, but I refuse to change my appearance. My most embarrassing moment was on a flight no less. I was coming back from Vancouver and as usual I was sitting at the front of the plane. Row 1 Seat A. I request to be seated at the front of the plane always because it makes getting off the plane so much easier. In any case, as I was the last one to get on the plane I took my seat at the front of the plane and I noticed a lot of the passengers staring at me. As I took my seat I could literally feel the stares of people sitting beside me and behind me. After about 30 seconds of tension, the flight attendant asked me to move. "Sir, perhaps you would be more comfortable at the back of the plane," she asked. In my mind I thought "Maybe you'd be more comfortable with me at the back of the plane." But instead of starting something on a plane I picked up my carry-on baggage and moved to the back of the plane. The plane was more than half empty and I was moved to the very last seat at the back of the plane. After landing in Edmonton, I was the last person to get off the flight and it felt like the flight attendant blew a sigh of relief, thanking God that I hadn't hijacked the plane! After that day I try to avoid taking that airline if I can help it, but I'll never forget the feeling of being treated like a criminal simply because I looked like a terrorist. (Baptized Sikh, male, University of California Los Angeles, 2004)

In the following excerpt, an Iranian student not only feels the persecution at a personal level but also understands what is going on at an institutional level. The passage of the Patriot Act and required registration by the INS has resulted in the detainment and persecution and loss of jobs for many innocents.

> At this moment, I cannot find words that articulate the frustration that I feel every time I am stopped at an airport terminal for "random security check" of my luggage/car or asked as to what *jihad* means. And I feel especially disconcerted when I find that the prejudice against Middle Easterns has not ceased, rather it has merely become subtle and more importantly institutionalized—the Patriot Act and special registration that the INS required of the immigrants from Islamic countries. The implementation of various laws hid under the guise of the protection of freedom for its veritable purpose was to seek out all people of Middle Eastern or South Asian descent who were Muslim and therein permitted discrimination based on religion or race. (Irani, female, University of California Los Angeles, 2003)

Racial profiling and hate crimes serve to destroy the family structure and financially weaken the ethnic communities. The civic population, who feel the need to paint individuals whom they believe to be different, threatens the livelihood of Middle Eastern and South Asian entrepreneurs. In the following excerpt, a Pakistani male describes the financial hardships faced by his uncle as well as his family friend. Despite the quality of their service, their profits waned merely due to their ethnic names and accents. They are forced to become enterprising and adopt various strategies to increase profits once again.

> My uncle, the owner of a convenience store in San Diego, began to receive threatening phone calls just days after the attacks on 9/11. The callers threatened the physical well-being of my uncle as well as members of his family. On one particular day, a Caucasian male in his late twenties drove up to the store in his pickup truck and shot at the windows with a gun. Although this incident did not cause any physical injuries, my uncle was so incredibly frightened by this incident that he closed the store for a week. Currently, the retaliatory behavior is not nearly as horrific, however, my uncle has definitely noticed a major decrease in business and therefore presently considering relocating his store. Incidentally, another family friend has also noticed a decline in his business. He owns a pool building company, and takes pride on the competitive rates, and the high level of service they offer. According to him, the fiscal performance of the business was excellent prior to 9/11. However, the business owner's name is Mohammad and it appears as though good service and great prices are no longer the determining factor in consumer's decision-making process. You see this individual relies on the yellow pages to drive his business. His company had quite an attractive leader ad in the yellow pages. He continues to

receive a high volume of calls; however, when the callers realize that the owner speaks with a thick Middle Eastern tongue, and is named Mohammad, they just simply hang up, or say that they will call back. As you can probably well imagine, they never call back. Business had been facing a decline, so this individual hired a very well-spoken Caucasian as his receptionist, who is responsible for answering the phones and scheduling appointments. Ironically, business is thriving once again. (Pakistani, male, California State University Northridge, 2003)

As the backlash towards the South Asian and Middle Eastern communities increased, the U.S. Department of Justice (Civil Rights Division) was requisitioned by the Bush administration to vehemently prosecute the perpetrators. Ironically, beginning September 17th, 2001, the U.S. government initiated more than 27 programs that condoned religious and ethnic profiling so as to apprehend terrorists that might have entered the country as part of its "War on Terrorism" policy. These initiatives gravely affected the immigrant families, namely the South Asian and Middle Eastern communities, for many were detained in INS prisons, interviewed, and deported back to their homeland.[2] As the student testimonies show, these policies subtract from the already limited rights of immigrants. In the following excerpt, a Bangladeshi female expresses the tumult her family experienced due to these policies. When the student's family makes a donation to a nonprofit Islamic organization during the holy month of Ramadan, when Muslims are required to give *zakath,* the FBI places them under surveillance and monitors their every move, thereby threatening the mobility and financial stability of the family.

> The months following the attacks on the World Trade Center on September 11th, 2001 was an incredibly tumultuous time for my family. Every year, we give *zakath* (donation) for as Muslims we are required to give a certain percentage of our earnings to the needy. My mother and grandmother thought it best to donate to a nonprofit organization that provides aid to refugees in various Islamic countries. A few weeks after the attacks, my father's bank accounts were "frozen." The Federal Bureau of Investigation began to investigate him for possible ties with terrorist organizations. Although my father vehemently denied any such affiliation, he was taken in for questioning. They informed my father that he had written checks for large amounts to a nonprofit organization that was currently facing charges for aiding terrorists. After hours of reiterating that my mother had written those checks as *zakath* during the month of Ramadan the investigators allowed him to leave. They informed him they did not ac-

---

[2]Bakalian, A., & Bozorgmehr, M. *Government initiatives after the September 11th attacks on America. Encyclopedia of Racism in the United States.* Westport, CT: Greenwood Press.

quire any discriminating information regarding my family via wire-tapping and exploring personal e-mails. However, they were certainly going to maintain their vigilance in regards to accumulating information on possible dealings with terrorist cells. They also required us to obtain their clearance for interstate travel and we were prohibited from traveling out of the country. The airport security measures were already quite stringent for they profiled South Asians for "random baggage checks" but a security clearance was an extremity. This measure especially affected my father who happened to travel a great deal for business. On several occasions, my father missed the connecting flight to his destination for the FBI failed to clear him on time. The financial repercussion of this was substantial for he incurred added expenses for flying (security clearance by the FBI often took a long time) and missed business opportunities due to the delays. This also created a stressful environment at home: We were petrified of mistakenly saying anything that might somehow indicate that we were "unpatriotic." The very mobility of our family was circumscribed and a cloud of suspicion hung over our heads. And we became increasingly isolated and confined in the country where we were born and raised by virtue of being South Asian and Muslim. (Bangladeshi, female, California State University Northridge, 2004)

In the following excerpt, an Afghani female explains the affect of painting on her family and friends. The hatred extends beyond racial slurs to physical violence directed towards members of ethnic communities who are threatened at gunpoint and stabbed. The student also understands that the backlash is permitted at an institutional level through the various policies that threaten the mobility and freedom of these individuals.

My interactions with my family and friends have allowed me a glimpse of the extent of the damage that has been done to the South Asian community as of 9/11. The devastating effects of profiling and hate crimes have risen to cause severe physical, psychological as well as financial injury. A close friend of the family, who operates a business in the Downtown Los Angeles area, has been beaten and stabbed following the attacks on the World Trade Center. A friend, who operated a few stores in the Southern California area, was forced to shut down his business for an extensive period due to community members who threatened him at gunpoint. The community "patriots" felt it was "unjust that a terrorist should profit from their neighborhood." The lack of income lead to the demise of the business; causing him to shut down the stores altogether. Also, the special registration mandated by the INS was quite injurious to the South Asian community for it lead to the deportation and imprisonment of various individuals, while others were restricted from leaving the country. In one particular instance, a friend of the family was disallowed from leaving the USA even when his family members, who lived in Afghanistan, passed away. The feelings of helplessness are often overwhelming. Although the attacks caused an increase in the number of hate crimes and state violence, it certainly would be naïve to imply that these acts were merely due to the attacks. Rather, it allowed for the dramatic expression of vile thoughts. Even the pleas made by the Bush administration to stop hate crimes and the harsh prosecutions of criminals who commit such crimes are not enough, especially when racial profiling by security officials in airport terminals follows them! Members of my family have not only been selected for "random" baggage searches but airport officials have also detained them for 2–3 hours of questioning. (Afghani, female, California State University Northridge, 2003)

Stories about hatred, insults, economic discrimination, and state violence are not the ultimate form of racism. The ultimate form is murder. The loss of a loved one has a tremendously devastating impact on the family and friends. One of our students has to deal with the loss of her uncle due to the hatred and anti-Muslim fervor that continues to rip through America and Americans.

The country I live in taught me how to discriminate, hate, and judge those who are different. It is a country that requires its citizens to fit into a mold. If they deviate, they are deemed fanatical, nonconforming, and erroneous. However, the problem is that the country in which I live is the United States of America and the people that are victimized, criticized, and seen as different are my people and I. After the attacks on September 11th, 2001, we as a country stood together with patriotism in our hearts and revenge on our minds. We united against the evil that caused our demise. However, I was unaware that we classified evil solely on the basis of physical appearance. If I had known I would have been a good American and tried to prevent the terror by turning in my family. I would have arrested all baptized Sikhs, who wear the ceremonial sword symbolic of fighting injustice and protecting the weak. I would have thrown rocks at my father, my uncles, and my brothers because the turban that they wear, which symbolizes a rise against oppression, reminds this country of Osama Bin Laden. Finally, I would have shot the convenient storeowner, who is my uncle. The impact of this murder still affects me. Whenever a male friend or family member, who wears a turban and has unshorn hair, accompanies me I receive either a cold stare or a hateful comment. (Sikh, female, CSUN, 2003)

Like many subordinates that you have read about, the Middle Eastern and South Asian students have not given up on the United States. The reasons that they and their families came here still remain in their hearts. This student describes the hope that she holds.

It is my hope that this country can go back to normal and that we can get rid of the various acts that discriminate on the basis of race and religion. I am still hopeful, though, and believe that this is a good country to live in. (Pakistani, female, University of California Los Angeles, 2004)

Beyond hope there is also action that seeks to create the change they so desire for themselves and their families despite the threat of repercussions. In the following excerpt, a Sri-Lankan female, who is made to feel very uncomfortable about her adherence to Islam, wonders about her choice. Although she was made to feel bad about being a Muslim, she embarks upon a journey that seeks to inform her fellow Americans about the virtues of Islam.

My quest to discover my religion, which was deemed "evil" by the populace, led me to be more proactive and become involved in raising awareness about the goodness of Islam in the Southern California area. However, my parents insisted that I become vigilant regarding my actions and speech in apprehension that our phone, e-mail, and household as a whole were being surveyed by intelligence agencies. They further urged me to refrain from going out and to be cautious of my surroundings, especially in the days following the attacks in New York because they were certain that there would be retaliation from "patriotic Americans." I also noticed various family members and friends of South Asian descent, who strategically placed the American flag in front of their house and in their car to protect against any assumption of "unpatriotic feelings." The trepidation was apparent in every action—my parents refused to discuss the attacks, refrained from going to the *mosque* on Fridays, avoided traveling out of town, and even avoided going to work for a few days. You see it was not too long ago that the Japanese were confined to internment camps, they said. They had immigrated to this Land of Freedom with the knowledge that they would be able to escape persecution, however this event had revealed the illusion for what it truly is. (Sri-Lankan, female, University of Southern California, 2003)

Middle Eastern South Asians and Muslims are not the only ones responsible for the education of those who are ignorant and frightened. Hate crimes and discrimination will diminish when dominants act to prevent or stop religious and ethnic persecution. In the following example, a White, Christian manager takes such an action. In a scene described earlier in this chapter, a customer in a bank refuses to be served by a Persian female teller and challenges the manager for employing "such people."

My manager then advised her to leave and refrain from transacting at the branch if she could not appreciate her tellers. It so happened that my manager was also a middle-aged Caucasian woman and it was in her conviction that I found strength again. I was afraid to speak out against the ignorant comments made by the customer for it might endanger my job or lead to other forms of retaliation. Apprehensive of what others might say, I had secluded myself as though I was shamed of my religion or my culture. (Persian, female, California State University Northridge, 2003)

# CONCLUSION

As stated earlier, our students were truly heroic. They exposed themselves to pain, and committed to learn from others and about others. More importantly, they learned from others about themselves. However, it would be a mistake to consider this an astounding accomplishment. The students in the classes were hungry to talk and write about racism. No one had ever encouraged them. No one had ever let them believe that it was possible for genuine dialogue and understanding to occur. This class illustrates just how it is possible and profoundly necessary.[3] The voices you have heard throughout this book are gifts; they are the gifts of openness to the pain and hope of youth in America who are being raised in a racist society.

**Suggested Readings**

1. Bakalian, A., & Bozorgmehr, M. *Closure of Muslim philanthropic organizations after 9/11. Encyclopedia of Racism in the United States.* Westport, CT: Greenwood Press.
2. Bakalian, A., & Bozorgmehr, M. *Responding to the backlash by Arab/Muslim American advocacy organizations. Encyclopedia of Racism in the United States.* Westport, CT: Greenwood Press.

# STUDENT TESTIMONIALS

*Voices of Pain and Voices of Hope* explicitly shows the deep-rooted struggles of individuals who cannot fit the mold of a White, middle-class man. I used to dream that one day I could be part of the "superior" mold to escape adversity based on the tone of my skin color, the color of my hair, or the country I was born in. This book gives me the power to fight the racism instead of conforming to it. There are so many rich cultures and personalities eradicated to escape racism and the experiences in this book are just a drop in the ocean of pain that is inflicted in our society every day. Yet these experiences are gems for us to take to heart and understand what our society is and the cancer of racism that we must fight against. This book validates my struggles and gives me the strength to not sacrifice my name, looks, attitude, desires, and beliefs for the satisfaction of the ignorant.

> **Evish Kamrava, Iranian, Male, B.S. Biochemistry, University of California, Los Angeles, M.S. Physiology, Georgetown University**

---

[3]A film based on this class is being prepared by Professor J. Rabow and Evan Leong.

# REFERENCES

Blumenthal, S. (1994). The Christian soldiers. *The New Yorker,* July 7, 31.

Bobo, L. D. (1997). *Civil rights and social wrongs: Black-White relations since World War II.* In J. Higham (Ed.), Pennsylvania: Pennsylvania State University Press.

Bobo, L. D., & Hutchings, V. L. (1996). Perceptions of racial group competition: Extending Blumer's theory of group position to a multiracial social context. *American Sociological Review, 61,* 6, December, 951–972.

Bradshaw, C. K. (1992). Beauty and the beast: On racial ambiguity. In M. P. P. Root (Ed.), *Racially mixed people in America* (pp. 77–90). California: Sage Publications.

Chesler, M., & Peet, M. (2002). White student views of affirmative action on campus. *The Diversity Factor, 10*(2), 21–27.

Cose, E. (1993). *The rage of a privileged class.* New York: Harper Collins.

Diamond, J. (1999). *Guns, germs, and steel: The fates of human societies.* New York: W.W. Norton & Company.

DuBois, W. E. B. (1903/1995). *The souls of Black folk.* New York: Signet.

Duster, T. (1992). *The Diversity Project.* Berkeley, CA: Institute for the Study of Social Change, University of California, Berkeley.

Duster, T. (1993). The diversity of California at Berkeley: An emerging reformulation of "competence" in an increasingly multicultural world. In R. Thompson & S. Tyagi (Eds.), *Beyond a dream deferred: Multicultural education and the politics of excellence.* Minnesota: University of Minnesota Press.

Essed, P. (1991). *Understanding everyday racism: An interdisciplinary theory.* California: Sage Publications.

Ezekiel, R. S. (1995). *The racist mind: Portraits of Neo-Nazis and Klansmen.* New York: Viking Books.

Feagin, J. R. (1991). The continuing significance of race: Antiblack discrimination in public places. *American Sociological Review, 56*(1), 101–116.

Feagin, J. R. (2000). *Racist America: Roots, current realities, and future reparations.* New York: Routledge.

Freire, P. (1973). *Education for critical consciousness.* New York: Seabury Press.

Freire, P. (1994). *Pedagogy of the oppressed.* New York: Continuum.

Gerschick, T. J. (1995). Should and can a White, heterosexual, middle-class man teach students about social inequality and oppression? One person's experience and reflections. In *Multicultural Teaching in the University* (p. 200). Prager.

Hacker, A. (1992). *Two nations: Black and White, separate, hostile, unequal.* New York: Simon and Schuster.

Hacker, A. (1998). Grand illusion. *New York Review of Books,* June 11.

Helms, J. E. (1990). *Black and White racial identity: theory, research, and practice.* Connecticut: Greenwood Press.

Helms, J. E. (1992). *A race is a nice thing to have: A guide to being a White person or understanding the White persons in your life.* Kansas: Content Communications.

Hirschfeld, L. A. (1996). *Race in the making: Cognition, culture, and the child's construction of human kinds.* Massachusetts: MIT Press.

Howard, R. G. (1999). *We can't teach what we don't know: White teachers, multiracial schools.* New York: Columbia University Teachers College Press.

Hurtado, S., Milem, J., Clayton-Pedersen, A., & Allen, W. R. (1999). *Enacting diverse learning environments: Improving the climate for racial/ethnic diversity in higher education.* ASHE-ERIC Higher Education Report, Washington, DC: The George Washington University, Graduate School of Education and Human Development, Volume 26, No. 8., 133.

Illich, I. D. (1971). *Celebration of awareness: A call for institutional revolution.* New York: Doubleday.

Iwata, E. (1994). Race without face. *San Francisco Focus,* May 1991, 50–57.

Jackson, B. W. (1974). Black identity development. In L. Golubschick & B. Persky (Eds.), *Urban social and educational issues.* Iowa: Kendall/Hunt.

Judt, T. (1994). The lost world of Albert Camus. *New York Review of Books,* June 23, VXL VIII, No. 9, 6.

Kich, G. K. (1992). The developmental process of asserting a biracial, bicultural identity. In M. P. P. Root (Ed.), *Racially mixed people in America* (pp. 304–317). California: Sage Publications.

Kinder, D. R., & Sanders, L. M. (1996). *Divided by color: Racial politics and democratic ideals.* Illinois: University of Chicago Press.

Kinder, D. R., & Sears, D. O. (1981). Prejudice and politics: Symbolic racism versus racial threats to the good life. *Journal of Personality and Social Psychology, 40,* 414–431.

Lee, S. J. (1996). *Unraveling the "model minority" stereotype: Listening to Asian American youth.* New York: Teacher's College Press.

Lynd, R. S. (1939). *Knowledge for what? The place of social science in American culture.* New Jersey: Princeton University Press.

McIntosh, P. (1998). White privilege. In P. S. Rothenberg (Ed.), *Race, class and gender in the United States.* New York: St. Martin's Press.

McLaren, P. (1998). *Life in schools: An introduction to critical pedagogy in the foundations of education.* New York: Longman Publishers.

Miller, J. B. (1998). Domination and subordination. In P. S. Rothenberg (Ed.), *Race, class and gender in the United States.* New York: St. Martin's Press.

Nieto, S. L. (1996). *Affirming diversity: The sociopolitical context of multicultural education.* New York: Longman Publishers.

O'Brien, J., & Kollock, P. (2001). *The production of reality.* California: Pine Forge Press.

Orcutt, J. D. (1996). Teaching in the social laboratory and the mission of SSSP—Some lessons from the Chicago School. *Social Problems, 43*(3), August, 235–245.

Rabow, J. R., Radcliff-Vasile, S., Charness, M. A., & Kipperman, J. (1999). *Learning through discussion.* Illinois: Waveland Press.

Rabow, J. R., Stein, J. M., & Conley, T. D. (1999). Teaching social justice and encountering society: The pink triangle experiment. *Youth & Society, 30*(4), 483–514.

Richardson, T., Reyes, N., & Rabow, J. (1998). Homophobia and the denial of human rights. *Transformations, 9*(1), 68–82.

Rockquemore, K. A., & Brunsma, D. L. (2002). *Beyond Black: Biracial identity in America.* California: Sage Publications.

Root, M. P. P. (1996). A Bill of Rights for Racially Mixed People. *The multicultural experience: Racial borders as the new frontier.* California: Sage Publications.

Rothenberg, P. S. (1998a). *White privilege: Essential readings on the other side of racism.* New York: Worth Publishers.

Rothenberg, P. S. (1998b). *Race, class and gender in the United States.* New York: St. Martin's Press.

Said, E. W. (1978). *Orientalism.* New York: Vintage Books.

Sampson, E. E. (1999). *Dealing with differences: An introduction to the social psychology of prejudice.* Florida: Harcourt College Publishers.

Schuman, H., Steeh, C., Bobo, L., & Krysan, M. (1997). *Racial attitudes in America: Trends and interpretations.* Massachusetts: Harvard University Press.

Searle, J. R. (1993). Is there a crisis in American higher education? *Bulletin of the American Academy of Arts and Sciences, 1,* 24–27.

Sears, D. O., & Kinder, D. R. (1985). On conceptualizing and operationalizing "group conflict." *Journal of Personality and Social Psychology, 48,* 1141–1147.

Sears, D. O., Hensler, C. P., & Speer, L. K. (1979). White's opposition to "busing": Self-interest or symbolic politics? *American Political Science Review, 73,* 369–384.

Smelser, N. J., Wilson, W. J., & Mitchell, F. (2001). *America becoming: Racial trends and their consequences. Volume I.* Washington, DC: National Academy Press.

Smith, P. (1990). *Killing the spirit: Higher education in America.* New York: Viking Penguin.

Sniderman, P. M., & Carmines, E. G. (1997). *Reaching beyond race.* Massachusetts: Harvard University Press.

Solorzano, D. (1998). Critical race theory, racial and gender micro-aggressions, and the experiences of Chicana and Chicano scholars. *International Journal of Qualitative Studies in Education, 11*(1), 121–136.

Spickard, P. R. (1989). *Mixed blood: Intermarriage and ethnic identity in twentieth-century America.* Wisconsin: University of Wisconsin Press.

Spickard, P. R. (1992). The illogic of American racial categories. In M. P. P. Root (Ed.), *Racially mixed people in America* (pp. 12–23). California: Sage Publications.

Stewart, J. B. (1997). Coming out a Chrysler. *The New Yorker,* July 21, 38–50.

Takaki, R. (1993). *A different mirror: A history of multicultural America.* Massachusetts: Little Brown & Co.

Takaki, R. (1998). *A larger memory: A history of our diversity with voices.* Massachusetts: Little Brown & Co.

Tatum, B. D. (1997). *Why are all the Black kids sitting together in the cafeteria? And other conversations about race.* New York: Basic Books.

Thernstrom, S., & Thernstrom, A. (1997). *America in Black and White: One nation, indivisible.* New York: Simon and Schuster.

Tolerance.org. Tolerance in the news, bias 101. Retrieved November 21, 2001 from http://www.tolerance.org/news/article

Wolfe, A. (1998). *One nation, after all: What middle-class Americans really think about: God, country, family, racism, welfare, immigration, homosexuality, work, the right, the left, and each other.* New York: Viking Press.

Wright, R. (2001). The ethics of living Jim Crow: An autobiographical sketch. In P. S. Rothenberg (Ed.), *Race, class, and gender in the United States* (pp. 21–30). New Jersey: Worth Publishers.

# AUTHOR INDEX

**149**